But let the wood wind flutes begin,
Their elfin music, faint and thin,
I sway, I bend, retreat, advance,
And evermore—I dance! I dance!
Arthur Ketchum

RHYTHMS AND DANCES

for

ELEMENTARY SCHOOLS

GRADES ONE TO EIGHT

COMPILED BY

DOROTHY LA SALLE

First Assistant in Health Education, Detroit Public Schools

NEW YORK

A. S. BARNES AND COMPANY

1939

TO

MARY PATRICIA O'DONNELL

WHOSE FRIENDSHIP HAS EVER BEEN AN INSPIRATION

THIS BOOK IS DEDICATED

NOTE

This material was first published for the author by the Board of Education, Detroit, Michigan, as "A Course of Study in Rhythms and Dances for Elementary Schools."

TABLE OF CONTENTS

This book if used in conjunction with

PLAY ACTIVITIES
for Elementary Schools
by the same author

forms a comprehensive course of
study in Physical Education for the
elementary schools

ACKNOWLEDGMENTS

IT would be impossible for me to make fitting acknowledgments to the many people who have helped me in the preparation of this course of study. I am especially indebted to Mr. Norton H. Pearl, whose foresight and vision have been a constant inspiration, and to Mr. Loren M. Post, who as head of the Health Education Department (Detroit), has guided me by his helpful suggestions and criticisms. To Miss Ruth H. Sims, who read and corrected the entire manuscript, and assisted in its rearrangement, and to Miss Helen F. Webb Jones, who criticized and corrected the music, I wish to express my deepest gratitude.

I wish also to express my appreciation of the untiring effort of the following committee of teachers who gave their time and the value of their experience in the collection of this material: Miss Florence Albert, Mrs. Sara Baumgartner, Miss Marie Heghinian, Miss Dorothy Hyne, Miss Ruth Loebenstein, Miss Jane Mayer, Mrs. Marion Mayer, Mrs. Marion Rogers, and Mrs. Charlotte Westerman.

I am indebted to Miss Mary P. O'Donnell for a number of rhythms worked out in her classes; to Mr. J. H. Trybom, who so kindly translated several Scandinavian dances; and to the members of the Health Education staff of the Detroit Public Schools. The dances "Caribou" on page 79 and "Hopi Corn" on page 83 are reproduced with the permission of the Woodcraft League of America, from their manual, "The Birch Bark Roll."

DOROTHY LA SALLE.

SINGING GAMES ON THE PLAYGROUND

Rabbit in the Hollow

Draw a Bucket of Water   London Bridge

GIANTS

INTRODUCTION

DANCING is man's primitive and natural means of self expression. It is the most exuberant utterance of the joy of life.[1] Man has always danced. He jumped and leaped into the air, he skipped, and hopped, and gestured even before he had any written language. Every important phase of life was portrayed or celebrated in the dance. The ceremonial dance of primitive tribes was a type of prayer. When a tribe wanted a thing they danced for it. They danced to call the rain spirits to water their crops. They danced to bring food to the tribe in time of famine. When the men were away fighting the women danced daily to give courage to their warriors. Even among European peasants this religious significance was given to dancing, and until comparatively recently in certain sections of central Europe it was believed that the height of the corn depended upon the height of the leaps in the dance performed after the grain was planted. Probably the oldest record of dancing comes from Egypt and authorities put its date at 6000 B.C. In Chinese literature we find poems about dancing and dancers as far back as 1100 B.C. In 800 B.C. Homer related a story in the Odyssey about two young warriors dancing for the entertainment of Odysseus in the palace of Alcinous. In Greece it was considered a great compliment from one warrior to another to say that he danced well. Among the well known inscriptions carved in the rocks on the island of Thera in the Ægean is the following: "Bathycles dances well. Eumelos is a perfect dancer." Likewise there are many references to dancing in the Bible, the best known of which is from Psalm 150, "Praise Him in the cymbals and dances; praise Him upon the strings and the pipes." Following the history of dancing through the centuries we find countless musical compositions for the dance by great composers. The gigue, the sarabande, the courante, the gavotte, the mazurka, the polonaise, and the waltz all show the important place the dance held in the realm of music and in the history of civilization. The minuet was so popular in the seventeenth, eighteenth and nineteenth centuries that it has been incorporated into the structure of that greatest of all musical compositions, the symphony.

Dancing, as the oldest of the arts, should be cherished in our schools. It should be cherished because it is the most democratic of the arts since it is the only art easily accessible to everyone. It should be cherished because it is the only art in which special abilities are not essential. It should be cherished because it is a joyous, wholesome, natural means of expressing the rhythmic instinct. Herein lies one of its greatest values. It is this joyous expression of the rhythmic instinct that gives it its great recreative value. It is this that makes the child radiant when he skips. It is this that makes the older person bouyant at the end of a dance. It is this spirit that we would have in our schools.

That dancing has health values is an established fact. One need only take part in the skipping, running, galloping, and animal rhythms, with the little children or go through the figures of an old fashioned country dance with the eighth graders to be conscious of an increased heart-rate with its resultant stimulation of respiration and circulation. Dancing carries with it all of the beneficial physiological results of rational exercise. Probably the most important of these, coming through the happy recreative influence of the dance, is an increased nervous control and poise of rare value in the rush of present day life.

[1] Ellis, Havelock.

Dancing should help children appreciate and love good music. The annals of music are full of compositions with dance themes. These should be chosen instead of the cheap blatant jazz of today, which undoubtedly has its place in present day life but which has no place in the elementary school gymnasium. Through hearing good music the children become familiar with it and in as much as dance steps are rarely completed or changed except with the completion of musical phrases they become aware of the close connection between dancing and music and begin to understand and apply the rudiments of musical composition.

America has been colonized and settled by immigrants from foreign nations. The process has been going on since the first colonists set foot in Virginia. There is not a country in Europe which has not contributed towards making America what it is. Unfortunately some of the best characteristics of these people have been temporarily lost. Especially is this true of their capacity for art, particularly folk-art, folk handcraft, folk music and folk-dancing.[2] Through folk-dancing children should learn to appreciate the fine things their foreign neighbors give to them. They should learn to appreciate that the immigrant can contribute more than his labor. They should learn to appreciate that the immigrant has as much to give us as we have to give him.

In the elementary school program the following types of dancing should be included:

1. Free rhythms (Skipping, running, etc.)
2. Natural
3. Folk (Correlating with other subjects wherever possible)
4. Clogging
5. Character (Jumping Jack, Base Ball Dance)

Of all these types probably the only one which is unfamiliar is natural dancing. People who have some slight familiarity with it feel that children flitting about barefooted in cheese cloth costumes are doing natural dancing. Cheese cloth and bare feet are not essentials. Any costume which will give freedom will answer as well, but a loose costume and no shoes are best. Natural dancing seeks to interpret a piece of music, an idea, or an emotion, through the natural movements of the body, such as walking, skipping, running, leaping and hopping. It must be free from posturings, posings, and studied positions of the hands, feet and body. It must be free from all that is not sincere.

[2] Burchenal, Elizabeth, "Folk Dancing as a Popular Recreation."

SUGGESTIONS FOR PRESENTATION OF RHYTHMS AND DANCES

1. Give the dance atmosphere. Give its purpose, its name, its nationality, and the location of the country from which it comes. Tell the children all you can about the people who live there. Show them the type of costume worn. Whenever possible have children bring pictures and costumes. Point out the similarities between this dance and other dances of the same nation which the children know.

2. Have the music played.

3. Describe and demonstrate the first step. If the rhythm is difficult have the children clap it.

4. Teach by musical phrases rather than by counts, i.e. "Slide to the right until the music changes," rather than "Eight slides to the right." If this proves difficult have children listen to the music and clap when they hear the change in the music.

5. Teach all steps except extremely simple ones in a slow tempo at first. Difficult steps such as the polka, schottische, waltz, and mazurka should be made familiar in rhythm work before they are presented in a dance.

6. As soon as one step is learned put it with other steps previously learned, thus preserving the continuity of the dance.

7. Introduce pantomime and dramatization based upon the children's ideas, in presenting the dramatic rhythm and the singing game.

8. Encourage freedom and a great variety of expression in all rhythms. Do not insist upon circles and lines.

9. Remind the children that their singing should be sweet and soft in singing games. If voices are not sweet, practice the music with the syllable "loo."

10. Review all dances often. The better known a dance is the more it is enjoyed.

It is difficult to say just how many dances should be taught in any specified time. This depends so much upon the skill of each individual class. In schools or grades where dancing has been comparatively untouched it is well to begin with much simpler dances than are given for that grade. Teachers must first experiment and discover what the children can do before planning the dancing program for the year. In most schools it will be necessary to start at the beginning with the rhythm work as few children have had more than the simplest skipping and running. For girls this should be continued through the eighth grade. Boys will not be interested beyond the fourth grade and in many cases not beyond the third grade. Dances intended for boys are included in the lists of dances in the upper grades. The boy's dance training should not cease completely but should be adapted to his characteristics.

The time allotted is approximately seventy minutes per week in grades one through four, and forty-five minutes in grades five through eight. The boys in grades five through eight should have twenty minutes per week.

ELEPHANTS

BIBLIOGRAPHY
History, Theory, Festivals and Pageantry

BEEGLE and CRAWFORD, Community Drama and Pageantry, Yale University Press, New Haven.

BURCHENAL, ELIZABETH, Folk Dancing as a Popular Recreation, G. Schirmer, Inc., New York.

CHAMBERS, ROBERT, Book of Days, J. P. Lippincott & Co., Philadelphia.

CHUBB, PERCIVAL, Festivals and Plays, Harper & Bros., New York.

DALCROZE, E. J., Eurythmics, Small Maynard & Co., Boston.

DALCROZE, E. J., Rhythm, Music and Education, Putnam, New York.

DICKSON, EDWARD R., Poems of the Dance, Knopf, New York.

ELLIS, HAVELOCK, The Dance of Life, Houghton Mifflin Co., Boston.

ELLIS, HAVELOCK, The Philosophy of Dancing, Atlantic Monthly, 1914.

EMMANUEL, MAURICE, The Antique Greek Dance, John Lane Company, New York.

ENCYCLOPEDIA BRITANNICA, Dancing.

FRAZER, J. A., The Golden Bough, Macmillan & Co., Ltd., London.

GARDINER, E. N., Greek Athletic Games and Festivals, Macmillan & Co., Ltd., London.

GENTHE, ARNOLD, The Book of the Dance, M. Kennerly, New York.

GROVE, LILLY, Dancing.

GULICK, L. H., Folk Dancing, Russell Sage Foundation. Vol. III, No. 118, Parts I, II.

GULICK, L. H., Healthful Art of Dancing, Doubleday, Page & Co.

HAIRE, FRANCES, The Folk Costume Book, A. S. Barnes & Co., New York.

HALL, G. S., Educational Problems, Vol. I, D. Appleton & Co., New York.

HARRISON, J. E., Ancient Art and Ritual, Henry Holt & Co., New York.

H'DOUBLER, MARGARET, The Dance and Its place in Education, Harcourt, Brace & Co., New York.

H'DOUBLER, MARGARET, A Manual of Dancing.

KINNEY, TROY and MARGARET, The Dance, Frederick A. Stokes & Co., New York.

LEE, JOSEPH, Play in Education, Chap. XX, XXI., Macmillan Co., New York.

MARSH, AGNES and LUCILE, The Dance in Education, A. S. Barnes & Co., New York.

NEEDHAM, MARY, Folk Festivals, B. W. Huebsch, New York.

O'KEEFE and O'BRIEN, A Handbook of Irish Dances, M. H. Gill & Son, Ltd., Dublin.

RICE, A Brief History of Physical Education, A. S. Barnes & Co., New York.

SHARP, CECIL, Country Dance Book—Introduction, Novello & Co., Ltd., London.

SHARP, CECIL, The Morris Book—Introduction, Novello & Co., Ltd., London.

TAFT, LINWOOD, The Technique of Pageantry, A. S. Barnes & Co., New York.

URLIN, ETHEL, Dancing, Ancient and Modern, D. Appleton & Co., New York.

VULLIER, GASTON, History of Dancing, D. Appleton & Co., New York.

WILLIAMS, J. F., Education of the Emotions through Physical Education, Teachers College Record, May 1920.

WILLIAMS, J. F., Organization and Administration, Physical Education—pp. 70–72, Macmillan & Co., New York.

Dance Material

ARNOLD, FRANCIS, Collection of Rhythms for the Home, Kindergarten & Primary. Willis Music Company, Cincinnati.

BURCHENAL, ELIZABETH, Folk Dances and Singing Games, G. Schirmer Inc., New York.

BURCHENAL, ELIZABETH, Dances of the People, G. Schirmer, Inc.

BURCHENAL, ELIZABETH, Folk Dances of Denmark, G. Schirmer, Inc.

BURCHENAL, ELIZABETH, Folk Dances of Finland, G. Schirmer, Inc.

BURCHENAL, ELIZABETH, Folk Dances of Old Homelands, G. Schirmer Inc.

BURCHENAL, ELIZABETH, National Dances of Ireland, A. S. Barnes & Co., New York.

BERQUIST, NILS, Swedish Folk Dances, A. S. Barnes & Co., New York.

BENTLEY, ALYS, Play Songs, Laidlaw Brothers, Chicago.

BONNIER'S PUBLISHING HOUSE, 561 Third Ave., New York, Lekstugan—Gamla Svenska Folkdansar (Swedish Folk Dances) Norske Folkdansar 2 vol. (Norwegian Folk Dances).

COLBY, GERTRUDE, Natural Rhythms and Dances, A. S. Barnes & Co.

CRAMPTON, C. WARD, The Folk Dance Book, A. S. Barnes & Co.

CRAMPTON, C. WARD, The Second Folk Dance Book, A. S. Barnes & Co.

CRAMPTON and WOLLASTON, The Song Play Book, A. S. Barnes & Co.

CRAWFORD, CAROLINE, Dramatic Games and Dances, A. S. Barnes & Co.

CRAWFORD, CAROLINE, Folk Dances and Games, A. S. Barnes & Co.

CRAWFORD and FOGG, Rhythms of Childhood, A. S. Barnes & Co.

CRAWFORD and FOGG, Choice Rhythms for Youthful Dancers, A. S. Barnes & Co.

ELLIOT, Mother Goose Songs My Children Love, Noble & Noble.

FORENINGEN TIL FOLKEDANSENS FREMME (Association for Promotion of Folk Dances, Copenhagen, Denmark), Danske Folk Danse (Danish Folk Dances).

FROST, HELEN, Clog and Character Dances, A. S. Barnes & Co.

FROST, HELEN, The Clog Dance Book, A. S. Barnes & Co.

FROST, HELEN, and STRICKLAND, LILY, Oriental and Character Dances, A. S. Barnes & Co.

GEARY, MARJORIE, Folk Dances of Czecho-Slovakia, A. S. Barnes & Co.

GOMME and SHARP, Children's Singing Games, 5 vol. (English), Novello & Co., Ltd., London.

HARDING, Collection of Jigs and Reels.

HILLAS and KNIGHTON, Athletic Dances and Simple Clogs, A. S. Barnes & Co.

HINMAN, MARY WOOD, Gymnastic and Folk Dancing, 5 vols., A. S. Barnes & Co.

HOFER, MARIE, Children's Singing Games, A. Flanagan Company, Chicago.

HOFER, MARIE, Music for the Child World, 3 vols., Clayton F. Summy, Chicago.

HOFER, MARIE, Popular Folk Games and Dances, A. Flanagan Company.

101 MAGYAR NEPDAL (101 Old Hungarian Folk Tunes), Babas & Fodor, 8149 W. Jefferson Ave., Detroit.

MARSH, AGNES and LUCILLE, The Dance in Education, A. S. Barnes & Co.

O'KEEFE and O'BRIEN, A Handbook of Irish Dances, M. H. Gill and Son, Ltd., Dublin, Ireland.

RYAN, Dances of Our Pioneers, A. S. Barnes & Co., New York.

SETON, ERNEST THOMPSON, The Birch Bark Roll of the Woodcraft League of America, Inc.

SHARP, CECIL, The Country Dance Book, Novello & Co., Ltd.

SHARP, CECIL, Country Dance Tunes, Novello & Co., Ltd.

SHARP, CECIL, The Morris Book, Novello & Co., Ltd.

SHARP, CECIL, Morris Dance Tunes, Novello & Co., Ltd.

SHARP, CECIL, The Sword Dance Book, Novello & Co., Ltd.

SHARP, CECIL, Sword Dance Tunes, Novello, & Co., Ltd.

SHIPPS and SMITH, Lithuanian Dances, Clayton F. Summy.

U. S. Ethnological Reports, Indian Games, Dances, Vol. VI, XIV, XX, XII, XXIII, XXIV.

GENERAL INDEX

MECHANICAL DOLLS

CLASSIFIED INDEX

AMERICAN DANCES

CZECHO-SLOVAKIAN DANCES

DANISH DANCES

ENGLISH DANCES

FRENCH DANCES

GERMAN DANCES

HUNGARIAN DANCES

INDIAN DANCES (North American)

IRISH DANCES

ITALIAN DANCE

NORWEGIAN DANCE

RUSSIAN DANCES

SCOTCH DANCES

SWEDISH DANCES

PART I

FUNDAMENTAL AND PANTOMIMIC RHYTHMS

Revised Record Numbers
Rhythms and Dances for Elementary Schools

Dance	Page	Victor	Columbia	Dance	Page	Victor	Columbia
Chimes of Dunkirk	42	21618	—	Gathering Peascods	95	20445	—
Did You Ever See A Lassie	43	21618	—	Sweet Kate	95	20444	—
Farmer in the Dell	44	21618		Highland Schottische	95	21616	—
London Bridge	47	20806	A3148	Knapspolska	99	No longer made	
Looby Loo	49	20214	A3148	Sellenger's Round	100	20445	—
The Muffin Man	50	20806		Little Man in a Fix	115	20449	
Sally Go Round	53	22356		Tinker's Dance	116	No longer made	
Nixie Polka	59	21685		Sicilian Circle	118	20639	
On the Bridge of Avignon	64	22356		Virginia Reel	119	20447	A3079
Roman Soldiers	66	21617		The Hatter	132	20449	
Bleking	69	20989	—	Irish Long Dance	134	No longer made	
Carrousel	70	20432	—	Birdie in the Center	144	9246	
Hansel and Gretel	70	21620	—	The Crested Hen	150	21619	
I See You	71	20432	A3041	Highland Fling	158	21616	A3000
A Hunting We Will Go	72	22356		Irish Lilt	161	21749	A3061
Seven Pretty Maids	73	No longer made	—			21616	
Captain Jinks	76	20638		Komarinskaia	164	81920	
Gustaffs Skoal	80	20988		St. Patrick's Day	164	21619	A3000
Minuet	85	1434		Plain Quadrille	165	20638	
Money Musk	87	20447				20639	
Pop Goes the Weasel	88	20151	—	Norwegian Mountain March	87		A3041
		20447		Butterfly, The	95		A3068
Seven Jumps	89	21617		Reap the Flax	116		A3001
Csebogar	93	20992		Laudunum Bunches	164		A3052

— *Indicates no change*

Fundamental and Pantomimic Rhythms
Grades One to Three

The following are to be used throughout the first three grades. Except in special instances where note has been made, the material may be taken up at the discretion of the teacher. In cases where the music is not printed, the reference given first is best.

Walking

Marches

Music references:

Surette "Marches for Use in Schools."

Hofer "Music for the Child World," vol. II, p. 20.

Arnold Collection for Home, Kindergarten, Primary," p. 24.

Chauve Souris "Parade of the Wooden Soldiers."

Grainger Children's March, "Over the Hill and Far Away."

Dolls- The fun in playing this is to represent the uncertainty as well as the mechanical character of the movement. Dolly almost falls over now and then, and at the end the spring is all unwound and- over she goes.

Music references:

Crawford and Fogg "Rhythms of Childhood," p. 51.

Crawford "Dramatic Games and Dances" p. 59.

Grieg "Norwegian Dance" op. 35.

Ducks- The little ducks waddle along with wings flapping. Once in a while their heads disappear looking for worms.

Music references:

Hofer "Music for the Child World" vol. II, p. 116.

Crawford "Dramatic Games and Dances" p. 15.

Bentley "Play Songs" p. 16

Elephants- Down the street the elephants swing with slow cumbersome steps, their trunks almost sweeping the ground.

Music references:

Crawford and Fogg "Rhythms of Childhood,"

Hofer "Music for the Child World" vol. II, p. 112

The Bear

Russian Folk Song

Bears - Old Bruno is fat and clumsy whether on all fours or doing tricks on his hind legs.

Music references:

Russian Folk Song "Brother Ivan"

Crawford "Dramatic Games and Dances" p. 43.

Bentley "Play Songs" p. 12

Giants - Fee Fi Fo Fum! Seven league boots and a great big club!

Music reference:

Crawford and Fogg "Rhythms of Childhood," p. 71.

Going to Church - Children imitate the reverent manner in which they go to church.

Music reference:

Crawford and Fogg "Rhythms of Childhood," p. 25.

High Stepping Horses - Proud and spirited, these horses step along with prancing gait and heads held high.

Music references:

Schumann "Bunte Blatter, op 99, "Scherzo"

Arnold "Collection of Rhythms for the Home, Kindergarten and Primary," p. 86.

High Stepping Horses

Schumann Op. 99 Scherzo (1841)

Indians - The tall, straight braves move along in a dignified way or crouch low for a sight or sound of the enemy.

Music references:

Indian War Dance

Crawford "Dramatic Games and Dances," p. 15.

Herbert "Natoma" Dagger Dance (near end of Act II.)

Drum or Tom-Tom with padded stick.

Indian Braves

On Tip-Toes
Music references:

Mosher "On Tip Toes"

Hofer "Music for the Child World" vol. II, p. 8 first part only.

Tip Toe

Mary Mosher

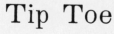
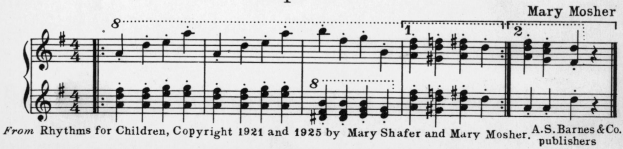

From Rhythms for Children, Copyright 1921 and 1925 by Mary Shafer and Mary Mosher. A.S. Barnes & Co. publishers

Skipping

Schubert - Ecossais

Skipping should be absolutely free with the arms swinging naturally at the sides. Emphasis should be placed on making the skip light and high rather than fast. Children should skip alone until they have sufficient skill to skip in groups. They should be permitted to skip anywhere they wish and not be made to skip in lines or circles.

Music references:

Crawford and Fogg "Rhythms of Childhood," p. 31.

Arnold "Collection of Rhythms for Home Kindergarten and Primary," p. 65.

Hofer "Music for the Child World," vol. II, p. 54.

Kerry Dance. See p. 132.

Nevin "Gondoliers Song."

Sharp "Green Sleeves."

Schubert "Moment Musicale."

Schumann "Album for the Young." Siciliano.

Sellengers Round. See p. 116.

Surette "Marches for Use in Schools." p. 46

Running

Schumann - Joyous Peasant

In running as in skipping, there will be a tendency on the part of some of the children to race. The emphasis should be placed upon running lightly in time to the music. At times it is wise to play very fast music, so that the children may run as fast as they wish.

Music references:

Hofer "Music for the Child World," vol. II, p. 3.

Crawford and Fogg "Rhythms of Childhood" p. 29.

Arnold "Collection of Rhythms," p. 68.

Surette "Marches for Use in Schools." p. 31.

Fairies

Have you seen the fairies dancing in the air,
And dashing off behind the stars to tidy up their hair?
I have, I have; I've been there!✱

Rose Fyleman

Mendelssohn Op. 61

Fairies – All children enjoy playing fairies. They love to steal out from under a blade of grass, running lightly and cautiously in fear of mortals. They whirl and run and dance until the first cock's crow sends them back to their hiding places.

Music references:

Crawford and Fogg "Rhythms of Childhood," p. 83

Hofer "Music for the Child World" vol. II, p. 6

Mendelssohn "A Midsummer Night's Dream." Fairies' March.

✱ *From* "Fairies and Chimneys" by Rose Fyleman, Copyright 1920, George H. Doran Company, Publishers.

Brownies

Music references:

Schumann "Phantasie"

Schumann "Pierrot" from "Carnival," op. 9.

Hofer "Music for the Child World," vol. II, p. 9.

Brownies

Schumann Op. 124, Elf

Leaves - Over the fields the leaves go dancing and whirling. When the wind (one of the children) dies down, the leaves settle quietly to the ground.   In season the same idea may be used for snowflakes.

Music reference:

   Crawford and Fogg "Rhythms of Childhood" p. 61.

   Crawford "Dramatic Games and Dances". p. 75.

Rolling Hoops-

Music reference:

   Hofer "Music for the Child World" vol. II, p. 90.

Tag - The phrasing of the music suggests just when to "Tag" and when the next child becomes "It."

Music reference:

   Hofer "Music for the Child World" vol. II, p. 14.

Trains - This idea may be worked out singly as locomotives or in groups as trains of cars. The train starts slowly and gradually goes faster and faster.

Music reference:

   Crawford and Fogg "Rhythms of Childhood" p. 61.

Trotting Horses

Schumann Op. 68 The Old Goblin

Trotting - The horses are off for a run with prancing and dancing!   At Christmas time time the idea of reindeers may be used.

Music reference:

Schumann "Children's Album," op. 68, The Old Goblin.

Hopping and Jumping

Children are apt to land heavily when jumping. Work for lightness, height, and a good landing on the balls of the feet.

Frogs - Just the word "Frog" will immediately bring forth suggestions of hopping and jumping from the children.

Music reference:

Hofer "Music for the Child World," vol. II, p. 110.

Jumping Jack - The movements should be suggested by the children after hearing the music played through once or twice.

Music reference:

Crawford and Fogg "Rhythms of Childhood," p. 55.

Sliding

A plain sideward slide may be made more interesting by facing in different directions with the change in the phrase of music, always continuing, however, in the line of direction. The change should be prepared for on counts 7 and 8 so that at the beginning of the new phrase the change has been made. At all times work for lightness and spring.

Music reference:

Surette "Marches for Use in Schools" p. 7.

Skating

Music references:

Hofer "Music for the Child World," vol. II, p. 122.

Arnold "Child Life in Music," p. 53.

Slide and Step

German Folk
Arranged by Mabel Jenkins

Three slides are taken followed by three steps in place with the knees high. The same idea in phrasing may be used with skipping followed by three walking steps.

Galloping

This should be made a very free and vigorous rhythm. Great care should be taken to see that the children gallop lightly on the toes.

Music references:

Hofer "Music for the Child World," vol. I, p. 86, vol. II, p. 68.

Godard "Postillon". (Unusually good.)

Arnold "Rhythms for the Home, Kindergarten, and Primary," pp. 77, 79, 85.

Schubert Ballet Music from "Rosamond".

Crawling

This rhythm may be used for bears or brownies.

Music references:

   Bentley, Play Songs "The Bear" p. 12

   Grieg "Hall of the Mountain King."

Whirling

Only a few measures of this should be played at a time for if continued long the children become dizzy.

Music reference:

   Crawford and Fogg "Rhythms of Childhood," p. 35.

Miscellaneous

See-Saw- With arms stretched sideward each child may act as a see-saw swaying from side to side to show the motion of the board. As partners, with both hands joined, they may ride on the board, alternately going up and down. In groups of three, the center child acts as the board and with arms outstretched, bends from side to side. The children on the outside alternately bend and stretch with the sway of the board.

Music reference:

   Hofer "Music for the Child World," vol. I, p. 109.

Swing- This is an excellent body exercise if the child really pushes the swing. It is a forward and backward rocking motion with hands stretched forward on the seat of the swing. At intervals the swing may be sent up with a great push as the child runs under it.

Music references:

   Hofer "Music for the Child World," vol. II, p. 85.

   Arnold "Rhythms for the Home, Kindergarten, and Primary," p. 101.

Rocking Horse- On all fours the children rock back and forth, or with one foot ahead of the other they rock from foot to foot. When on all fours the backs should not relax into a slump.

Music references:

   Crawford and Fogg "Rhythms of Childhood", p. 45.

   Hofer "Music for the Child World," vol. II, p. 96.

   Schumann, Album for the Young "On the Rocking Horse" p. 66.

Polka

Swedish Folk Dance Rillen

Polka

Schubert - Ecossais

Polka - Skip, run, run.
Music references:
   Folk Dance "Rillen."
   Beethoven "Turkish March."
   Scubert "Ecossaises."

FOURTH GRADE
Waltz Run

Schubert Tänze Op. 96 No. 15

Lightly

Waltz Run

Music references:

 Schubert "Tänze" op. 9b, N.º 15.

 Schubert "Tänze" op. 9a, N.º 3.

Accented Waltz Run

Music references:

 Schubert "Tänze" op. 9b, N.º 15.

 Schubert "Tänze" op. 9a, N.º 3.

Rhythms of the first three grades.

GRADES FIVE AND SIX

Leaping

Music references:

Surette "Marches for Use in Schools," p. 10.

Schubert "Marches" op. 40.

Leap, Run, Run

Music reference:

Hofer "Music for the Child World" vol. II, p. 8, second part.

Waltz Balance

Brahms

Waltz Balance - The waltz balance should be presented as follows:

1. Moving forward

2. Moving backward

3. Turning

Music references:

Brahms "Waltzes."

Schubert "Waltzes."

Rhythms of the preceding grades.

GRADES SEVEN AND EIGHT
Bouncing

Helen N. Smith

Bouncing - A series of eight little jumps are taken in place followed by four high jumps with back arched and arms stretched above head.

Music reference:

   Smith, Helen N. "Jumping Rhythm".

Ceremonial March - This should be the slow, dignified march of the processional used at such times as commencement, religious festivals, etc.

Music references:

   Hofer "Music for the Child World," vol. II, p. 38.
   Handel "Largo".

Circle Run -

Music reference:

   Colby "Natural Rhythms and Dances," p. 18.

Gallop, skip - For description of this skip see "Key to Directions" in music reference below.

Music reference:

   Colby "Natural Rhythms and Dances," p. 82.

High Skip

Music reference:

   Hofer "Music for the Child World," vol. I, p. 18.

Scarf Rhythm

Music reference:

   Hofer "Music for the Child World," vol. I, p. 12.

PART II

DANCE RHYTHMS

Dance Rhythms

In using rhythms with children it is desirable to give them every freedom of expression and to inspire them to create their own rhythms as soon as possible. For this reason only a few dance rhythms are presented as it is hoped that each teacher will guide her class towards this ideal.

GRADE ONE

My Dog

Hiller

Hollaender
Allegro con brio

Used by permission of Miss Ruth H. Sims.

Measures 1 - 8   A dog is playing with his little master.

He runs towards him.

,,   9 - 10   He jumps on his hind legs and begs.

,,   11 - 12   He looks up at his master and pants.

,,   13 - 24   Same as measures 9 -12.

,,   25 - 40   He chases his tail.

,,   41 - 44   He rolls on his back.

,,   45 - 48   He shakes himself.

On the last note he sneezes.

THE SEEDS GROW UP

Children pretend they are little seeds planted deep under the ground. They kneel on the ground curled up tightly, with their heads resting on their hands. Very, very slowly the children uncurl and rise to a standind position, as the seeds grow into tall willowy trees or pretty flowers that sway soft softly in the breeze.

It should be suggested to the children that their bodies represent the stalk of the flower or the trunk of a tree, and their heads the actual flower. Therefore, their heads should not be raised until they are standing nearly erect.

Music reference:
Hofer "Music for the Child World," vol. I, p. 14.

The reverse movement may be used to represent dooping flowers. Starting with heads, shoulders and arms drooping, the children gradually sink to the ground, curl up as before, or fall to the side as withered flowers.

Relaxation

R. Schumann, Op. 124, N⁰ 6

Enunciate the melody distinctly, play the triplet accompaniment lightly.

Statues

Old English Maypole Dance
Arranged by Louis Edgar Johns

STATUES

The children are in groups of five. One child is "It" and swings each of her four play-mates in turn, allowing them to fall into any pose they may choose. These may be beautiful, ugly, clownish, or animal statues. She then skips to the front of the group and tries to decide which one pleases her most. This decision requires closer inspection, however, and she skips to each statue in turn. None seem to please her and she shakes her head in disapproval of each. The disappointed statues sit up and watch her as she passes them by. Discouraged with the results she skips around in the center and finally falls into a pose she likes best.

"It" joins right hand with first child and turns her with a skip.	4 measures
Repeat with second, third, and fourth child	12 ,,
"It" skips to front to view statues.	4 ,,
"It" inspects the first statue and disapproves.	4 ,,
Repeat with others.	12 ,,
"It" skips to center and finishes in her chosen pose.	4 ,,

Used by permission of Esther Case Fox

Steps

Surprise Symphony
J. Haydn

STEPS

The children are in groups of eight. One child is "It", and stands about fifteen feet away from the other children with her back to them and her eyes covered. The rest of the group steal up from behind and try to reach "It" without being caught in action. In the meantime "It" pretends to count ten. She suddenly turns and catches them all moving. With a grand gesture she sends them back to the starting place. This time they are more cautious and and finally with great rejoicing reach the goal in safety.

"It" pretends to count. Children advance running but stop short as "It" turns around, "It" catches all.	2	measures
"It" watches them scurry back to the starting point.	2	,,
They advance as at first but no one is caught.	2	,,
Repeat but this time "It" sees them all moving just as they are about to reach goal and sends them back with a grand gesture.	2	,,
Some walk, some skip, some run back to start as "It" watches them gleefully.	4	,,
Move forward as at first but no one is caught.	2	,,
All dash to the goal clapping hands and jumping up and down as they successfully pass "It."	2	,,

Used by permission of Miss Mary P. O'Donnell

GRADE TWO
Shadows

A Shadow Dance
Elizabeth Rose Fogg

From Crawford "Dramatic Games and Dances" copyright 1914 by A.S. Barnes & Co., publishers.

During the first measure, the children walk slowly forward four steps watching to see the shadows move. On the second measure, they dash forward with little short running steps till the last note then they turn and look for the shadows again. On the third measure the movement repeats. During the fourth and fifth measures, they all turn to face the shadows and try to step on them — four very emphatic steps. During the sixth measure, they turn as at first, stretch to make themselves very tall and run forward very fast. At the seventh measure they make themselves as small as possible and run again. During the eighth and ninth measures, they turn and try to jump through their shadows with four long jumps.

Beginning with the tenth measure they all turn around, their backs to the shadows and walk proudly away, without one look behind. This little dance goes with much humor, for all children have tried these things over and over, and their enjoyment in telling the story is full of the mischief that anticipates the end of it all.

The Elves

Elfentanz
Edvard Grieg, Op. 12, N⁰ 4

Two elves, one older and serious, one younger and mischievous, come to the woods to make shoes. They look in all directions and assuring themselves that no one is there, the older one starts to work. The other elf, instead of working, teases his brother until in anger he chases him. He catches and scolds him, then orders him to work. The younger, not very intent upon his work, is quick to hear the sound of approaching steps. He tells his brother, they snatch up their tools and run away.

Measures 1 - 4   Enter first elf. Looks around.   Sees all is safe.
                      Beckons younger brother.

        5 - 8   First elf sits second elf down and makes him work.
                      First elf runs away to get tools.

      9 - 12   Younger elf throws down his tools and makes faces at brother.

   13 - 16   First elf returns, threatens his lazy brother, puts tools in his
                      hands and forces him to work.

   17 - 24   They both work. First elf has back turned toward his younger
                      brother.

   25 - 30   Younger elf becomes bored. He yawns, stretches, looks about for
                      amusement, and finally picks up a blade of grass.

   31 - 34   He tickles his brother's neck, laughs. Older brother thinking it
                      is a fly, slaps neck with hand and continues working.

   35 - 38   Second elf tickles his brother again. This time he is caught,
                      slapped by first elf and put to work again.

   39 - 44   Both work vigorously.

   45 - 46   Second elf puts his tools down quietly and tries to steal away.

   47 - 52   First elf sees him and chases him.

   53 - 60   First elf catches him and drags him back to work.

   61 - 64   Second elf becomes bored again, drops his work, yawns and
                      stretches.

   65 - 66   He hears a strange sound. Warns his brother.

   67 - 68   Both jump up frightened.

   69 - 72   Both run away.

Used by permission of Miss Frances Froatz and Miss Erma Oppenheimer

The Tight Rope Walker

W. A. Mozart
The Magic Flute

Allegretto

The Tight Rope Walker

The Tight Rope Walker bows formally to his audience, first to the left and then to the right. Balancing himself with a huge parasol he moves forward to the center of the rope, where he performs his more difficult stunts, first kneeling, then standing again to astonish his audience with a succession of quick springs from both feet. After this difficult feat he jumps to the ground and makes his final bow.

Bow to audience	2	measures
Walk to center of rope	8	,,
Kneel and rise	4	,,
Spring with right foot in front	1	,,
Spring with left foot in front	1	,,
Spring twice with right foot forward and twice with left foot forward	1	,,
Spring changing right, left, right, and left.	1	,,
Jump down and bow	2	,,

The Spring Fairies

The seeds lie scattered and in small groups. Rain Fairies, Sun Fairies (and any others the children may suggest) dance among the seeds, casting upon them their magic spell. (4 meas. repeated.) The seeds sprout and grow to be plants. After they have become tall flowers they sway softly in the breeze. (8 meas.) The fairies invite the flowers to dance with them. (4 meas.) The fairies and flowers dance, some individually and some in small groups, some running, some skipping, some twirling, but each doing what the music or idea prompts. At the end the flowers go back to their places and again become just ordinary flowers blooming in their beds. (Last 8 meas. played twice.)

Music reference:

Hofer "Music for the Child World" Vol. III Water Sprites.

Description used by permission of Miss Ruth H. Sims

GRADE THREE
Barnyard Squabble

Cedric W. Lemont
Barnyard Denizens No. 1
Cock-o-the-Walk

The first cock enters, proudly showing off his fine feathers.

Second cock equally proud enters.

First cock challenges the other to fight.

Second cock accepts.

They fight. (Fold arms in front, hop on either foot, and try to push one another over.)

First cock, self-satisfied, turns from his opponent and mocks him.

Second cock proudly protests.

First cock turns away with disgust.

Second cock indifferently goes in opposite direction.

Each walks away mocking the other.

Cock Walk - May be represented as follows:

Hands on hips, elbows back for wings; head and chest high; steps are taken with knees raised high.

Used by permission of Miss Riva Davidson and Mrs. Isabelle R. Octavec.

The Old Woman Who Lived in a Shoe

There Was An Old Woman
Elizabeth Rose Fogg

From Crawford's "Dramatic Games and Dances" copyright 1914 by A. S. Barnes & Co. Publishers.

The children are in a circle with one in the center to represent the old woman. During the first four measures they run excitedly about as if in some game and not paying any attention to the one in the center. At the fifth measure the center player pretends to beat them all soundly. They gradually become quieter until the ninth measure when all are still, and they are lying down peacefully sleeping, at the tenth measure.

To represent the confusion of the first four measures, it is necessary to have a very definite plan of action. Some of the players must go in a certain path following a leader and others in another. Until the teacher realizes that the more confused and complex the action, the greater the need of definite organization, it is better not to attempt this type of dramatization. On the other hand, it is one of the most vivid ways of training the expression of changed moods.

The Doll That Could Not Sleep

Theme from Sonata
W. A. Mozart

A little girl kneels at her doll's cradle and gently rocks it to and fro   The doll will not go to sleep. She tries to close its eyes with a deft forefinger.   This proving unsuccessful, she shows her bewilderment by pulling her own eyes open in imitation of the staring doll, and then continues to rock the cradle. (8 measures A music) Discouraged, she lifts the doll carefully from the cradle and places it in its carriage. She gently arranges the covers and screws the top securely into place. (Repeat 8 measures.) Then she wheels it slowly along stopping occasionally to run forward and peek at the sleepless one. (10 measures B music.) Returning from the last inspection her foot catches in the wheels and she falls, tipping the carriage over and breaking her doll. Kneeling, she slowly and sadly gathers up the fragments and puts them together in a tiny heap. (8 measures. Repeat B music.) She droops in utter dejection at her loss (2 measures.)

Used by permission of Miss Marjorie Mc Gowan.

PART III

DANCES AND SINGING GAMES

GRADE ONE
Blue Bird

Bluebird, bluebird, in and out my windows,
Bluebird, bluebird, in and out my windows,
Oh! Johnny, I am tired; Oh! Johnny, I am tired.

Take a little boy, and tap him on the shoulders,
Take a little boy, and tap him on the shoulders,
Oh! Johnny, I am tired; Oh! Johnny, I am tired.

When girls are chosen, sing "Oh! Jenny, I am tired" and "Take a little girl."

Formation - Single circle, facing center, hands joined high, making windows or archways.

Description -
Verse - Children sing while one child goes in and out the windows.
Chorus - The child chosen to be Bluebird stands behind one of the children in the circle and taps him on the shoulders with both hands, throughout the chorus. That child then becomes the leader, and the dance is repeated, while the other child follows behind with both hands on shoulders of the new leader. As the line increases, all tap shoulders of the person in front of them, as they sing the chorus. The dance continues until all are chosen.

Chimes of Dunkirk

Victor 17327- Columbia A-3061

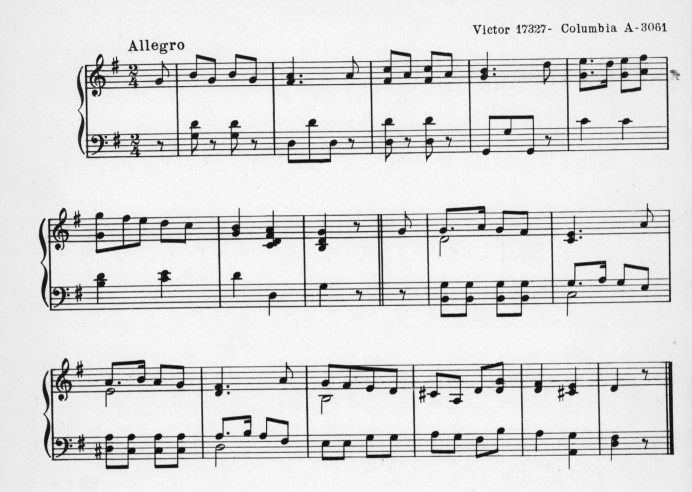

Oh! Come mark time with me,

And clap your hands in glee

And while the bells so sweetly ring,

Come dance with me.

Formation - Partners facing each other in single circle.

Measures 1 - 2 Stamp three times, right, left, right.

3 - 4 Clap three times.

5 - 8 Join hands with partner and turn around in place.

9-16 All join hands and run around in circle moving to left.

Repeat from beginning.

From Crampton "The Folk Dance Book," copyright 1909 by A. S. Barnes & Co; publishers.

Did You Ever See A Lassie

German

Victor 17568 - Columbia A- 3149

From Bancroft's "Games for the Playground, Home, School, and Gymnasium." Used by permission of the Macmillan Company, Publishers.

Did you ever see a lassie, a lassie, a lassie,

Did you ever see a lassie do this way and that?

Do this way and that way, do this way and that way,

Did you ever see a lassie do this way and that?

Formation - Single circle, hands joined with one child in the center.

Measure 1 - 8 Skip around to the left during the first two lines of the song. As the words "do this way and that" are sung, the child in the center imitates some activity.

"   9-16 All drop hands, face center of circle and imitate leader.

Encourage original suggestions from the children. "Laddie" is sung if a boy is chosen.

The Farmer in the Dell

English

Columbia A 2133

The farmer in the dell,
The farmer in the dell,
 Heigh-o the cherry-oh!
The farmer in the dell.

The farmer takes a wife,
The farmer takes a wife,
 Heigh-oh! the cherry-oh!
The farmer takes a wife.

The wife takes a child,
The wife takes a child,
 Heigh-oh! the cherry-oh!
The wife takes a child.

The succeeding verses vary only in the choice in each, and follow in this order:

The child takes a nurse, etc.
The nurse takes a cat, etc.
The cat takes a rat, etc.
The rat takes a cheese, etc.
The cheese stands alone, etc.

The players stand in a circle with one member in the center, who represents the farmer in the dell. At the singing of the second verse, the farmer beckons one into the circle, for his wife. The wife goes into the center and in turn chooses the child. This continues through the succeeding verses until the lines "The cheese stands alone" are sung. The players inside the circle and those forming it then jump up and down clapping their hands in a grand confusion and the game breaks up.

Atisket, Atasket

Arranged by Mabel Jenkins

Atisket, Atasket, a green and yellow basket,
I sent a letter to my love and on the way I dropped it, I dropped it,
          I dropped it,
A little boy picked it up and put it in his pocket, his pocket, his
          pocket,
A little boy picked it up and put it in his pocket.

Formation: Circle, hands joined.

One child, with handkerchief, runs around the outside of the circle and drops it behind any other child. The second child picks it up and chases the first child, who tries to run around the circle and return to the second child's place without being caught. If successful he is "It" again. If caught, the second child may be "It."

From "North Carolina Course of Study in Physical Education," used by permission.

I'm Very Very Tall

I'm very, very small
Or I'm very, very tall
Sometimes small, sometimes tall
Guess which I am now.

Description – The children are in a circle with one child in the center, who covers her eyes. Someone in the circle is chosen to tell them which they are to be - tall or small - at the end of the game. As they sing "I'm very, very tall" they all stretch up as high as ever they can. When singing "I'm very, very small" they make themselves as tiny as possible. They stretch up again as they sing slowly "sometimes tall" and down with "sometimes small." After a very short pause while the one named at the beginning of the game gives the signal for them all to be either tall or small, they sing quickly, "Guess which I am now!"

Little Ducks

Mary M. Mosher

Some little ducks a walk did take
Down the yard and past the gate
Into the pond as you shall learn
And out they pulled a worm.

Quackity, quack, quack, quack, quack, quack,
Quackity, quack, quack, quack, quack, quack,
Into the water down they go,
Just so!

Directions:

Verse I - The children waddle in imitation of a duck. During the last two lines of the first verse they put their heads down into the water, their arms backward to imitate the ducks' wings and jerk with their heads as though pulling out a worm.

Verse II - The ducks waddle about the room until the words "Into the Water down they go" when they bend their head forward and arms back as though swimming.

London Bridge*

2. Build it up with iron bars, etc.

3. Iron bars will rust away, etc.

4. Build it up with pins and needles, etc.

5. Pins and needles rust and bend, etc.

6. Build it up with penny loaves, etc.

7. Penny loaves will tumble down, etc.

8. Build it up with gold and silver, etc.

9. Gold and silver I have not got, etc.

10. Here's a prisoner I have got, etc.

11. What's the prisoner done to you, etc.

12. Stole my watch and broke my chain, etc.

13. What'll you take to set him free, etc.

14. One hundred pounds will set him free, etc.

15. One hundred pounds we have not got, etc.

16. Then off to prison we must go, etc.

Directions: Two players represent the bridge by joining hands and raising them so as to form an arch. The rest of the children in a single line, or in couples, pass under the bridge. When the words "My fair lady" are sung, the two keepers of the bridge let their arms fall, catching whichever child happens to be passing under at the time. He then is asked the question "Do you choose gold or silver?" The keepers have privately agreed which of these words each will represent, or if they wish they may decide upon other tempting prizes. The prisoner then stands behind the child representing his choice.   When all have been caught the game ends with a tug of war between the two sides.

From Hinman "Gymnastic and Folk Dancing" copyright by Mary Wood Hinman, A.S.Barnes & Co.,publishers

The Music Box

Now the music box will play,
Grandma took the key and wound it
All its tunes are bright and gay
Don't they mostly sound the same?

Grandma says 'twas made in France
That is where she said she found it.
Hear that queer old fashioned dance?
Amaryllis is its name.

Tra la la la la la la,
Tra la la la la la la,
Tra la la la lala la la,

Description- Half the children sit on the floor and pretend they are playing their music boxes, while they sing the above song. The rest of the children become the old-fashioned dolls pic - tured on their music boxes, and dance a little minuet. At the end of the song the groups change.

Music: Hofer "Music for the Child World" Vol. II, Air du Roi Louis XIII, p.129

Looby Loo

1. Here we dance looby loo, here we dance looby light,
Here we dance looby loo, all on a Saturday night.
Put your right hand in, put your right hand out,
Shake your right hand a little, a little,
And turn yourself about. Oh!

2. Here we dance looby loo, etc.
Put your left hand in, etc.

3. Here we dance looby loo, etc.
Put your right foot in, etc.

4. Here we dance looby loo, etc.
   Put your left foot in, etc.

5. Here we dance looby loo, etc.
   Put your little head in, etc.

6. Here we dance looby loo, etc.
   Put your whole self in, etc.

Formation: Single circle, hands joined.

Skip to the left until the words "Saturday night" are sung. All put right hands in towards center of circle, then stretch right hands away from center of circle. All shake right hands hard and turn in place. Repeat for following verses, suiting action to words.

Looby Loo*

*From Hinman "Gymnastic and Folk Dancing" copyright by Mary Wood Hinman, A.S. Barnes & Co., publishers.

The Muffin Man

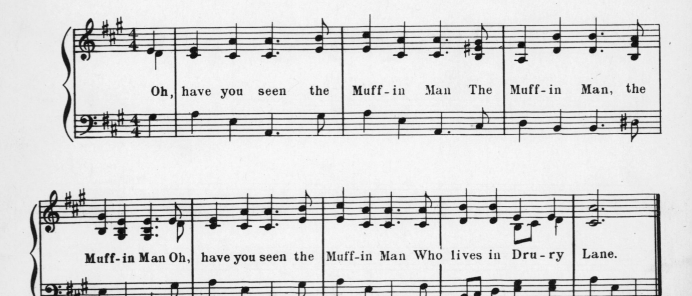

Oh, yes we've seen the Muffin Man
The Muffin Man, the Muffin Man
Oh yes we've seen the Muffin Man
Who lives in Drury Lane.

2. Two have seen the Muffin Man etc.

3. Four have seen the Muffin Man etc.

4. All have seen the Muffin Man etc.

One large circle with hands joined, skipping to the left. A child stands in the center and chooses a partner from out the big circle by skipping toward the chosen one and offering both hands on the words "Oh yes we've seen the Muffin Man." The two occupying the center now join both hands and sing "Two have seen the Muffin Man." to the end of this verse. At the beginning of the next verse these two choose partners from out the ring and the four join hands singing "Four have seen the Muffin Man." This is repeated until all are chosen, and the big circle sings "All have seen the Muffin Man." with the circle moving in the contrary direction.

Rabbit in the Hollow

German

Rabbit in the hollow sits and sleeps,

Hunter in the forest nearer creeps.

Little rabbit have a care:

Deep within your hollow there,

Quickly to the forest

You must run, run, run.

Formation - Circle, hands joined. One child chosen to be rabbit crouches in center; another, the hunter hides outside circle. Determine where rabbit's home is so that he may be safe.

Circle moves to the left during the first five lines. Stand still on last line while rabbit breaks through circle and tries to get home. If he succeeds he may be rabbit next time. If caught he must choose a new rabbit.

From "The North Carolina Course of Study in Physical Education." Used by permission.

Sailboat

French Folk
arranged by Mabel Jenkins

I had a little sail-boat
Its decks were new, and all painted blue.
I had a little sail boat and sailed it on the sea.
And sailed it on the sea.

An ugly frog sat staring
An ugly frog sat on a log
An ugly frog sat staring and leaped onto my boat.
And leaped onto my boat.

My boat went topsy turvy
Its sails so white disappeared from sight
My boat went topsy turvy and sank beneath the wave.
And sank beneath the wave.

Formation - Children scattered around room.

Verse I - With arms hanging parallel swing them gently from side to side.

Verse II - Crouch down, knees spread apart, hands on floor; sit staring, until the word "leaped," when all make a big leap forward.

Verse III - Stand again and swing arms as before but much more vigorously until the words "and sank beneath the wave" when children drop to the floor and lie quietly.

The words of this game are taken from "140 Folk Songs (Rote Songs) for Grades I, II, III Concord Series No. 7." Copyright 1921 by E.C. Schirmer Music Company. Used by permission.

Permission to use the game obtained from Mrs. Martha H. Wiest

Sally Go Round

D.C. ad lib.

Sally go round the moon
Sally go round the stars
Sally go round the chimney pots
Every afternoon - Bump!

Description - Hands joined in single circle formation. Starting with left foot circle moves clockwise with a skipping step singing the above lines. At the word "Bump" (to be sung crisply and loudly) all squat down. Without pause repeat stanza, dancing in opposite direction, starting with right foot. A variety of steps may be used, walking, skipping, sliding and running. In using a running step the song should be sung more quickly.

Shifty Shadows

1. Little flitting shifty shadow,

   I would like to fly with you;

   We will dance and skip together,

   Just what I do, you do too.

2. First we'll be a robin flying

   Spreading wide his big brown wings.

   Then we'll rest on waving tree tops

   While the robin sits and swings.

3. Here's a rabbit, shifty shadow

   See him wag his ears at you.

   Here's a little fish a swimming

   In the water deep and blue.

4. Here's a funny little Brownie

   Treading softly on his toes,

   Hurry, hurry, little shadow

   You must go where Brownie goes.

Verse 1. Children play with their shadows.

    ,,   2. Fly like robins, then rest on the tree tops imitating the swaying of the trees.

    ,,   3. Hop like rabbits. Run, moving hands in imitation of fish swimming.

    ,,   4. Crouch down and with softly treading feet, imitate brownies.

Used by permission of Mrs. Cora Jeffers

This is the Way the Lady Rides

1. This is the way the lady rides
    Gentle and slow, gentle and slow
    This is the way the lady rides
    All on a pleasant morning.

2. This is the way the gentleman rides
    Trotting along, trotting along, etc.

3. This is the way the farmer rides
    Joggity trot, etc.

4. This is the way the messenger rides
    Gallop along, etc.

Formation - Single circle or scattered about the room. Reins in left hands, crop in right.

1. Easy walk, lifting knees slightly.
2. Brisk, high stepping horses.
3. Slow clumsy gallop of farm horse.
4. Fast gallop, pull back hard and gradually slow down on last line.

The music should be played in such a way as to show the type of horse being por-trayed.

GRADE TWO
The Brownies Dance

Portuguese Folk
Arranged by Mabel Jenkins

Oh! as I was out a-walking in the wood, one night in June,
I came upon an open place dim lighted by the moon;
And within the misty circle was a troop of little men,
Dancing ring-around, and ring-around, and ring-around again.

They were funny little fellows with long beards as white as snow,
And each wore a scarlet, pointed cap with tinkling bells below;
To the music made by katy-dids and crickets in the night
They were capering and scampering and prancing with delight.

All at once I stepped upon a twig that crackled where I stood;
Like a flash the troop of tiny men slipped off into the wood;
And as far and farther yet they went I heard the music fade
Dying airily and fairily to silence in the glade.

Homer Harbour

It is suggested that the children create their own dance by dramatizing the words.

Elephants

Mary Morgan Mosher

The elephant's walk is steady and slow
His trunk like a pendulum swings just so
But when there are children with peanuts around
He swings it up and he swings it down.

Throughout the dance the body is in a relaxed, forward position swinging the arms as the trunk. The gestures should be very slow.

From "Rhythms for Children" Copyright 1925 by Mary Shafer and Mary Mosher. A.S. Barnes & Co., Publishers.

The King of the Barbarees*

English Singing Game

Arr. by Elizabeth Root

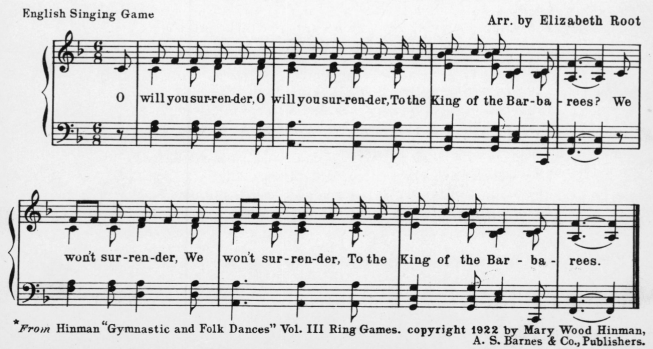

O will you sur-ren-der, O will you sur-ren-der, To the King of the Bar-ba - rees? We

won't sur-ren-der, We won't sur-ren-der, To the King of the Bar - ba - rees.

Children line up in couples. The first two face each other and join hands. These two represent the castle and step away from the others 6 or 8 feet. The next two separate and stand at either side of the couple behind them. This couple which is now in the center are the King and Queen, and the two outside children are the guards. The children still in couples back of the King and Queen are the trusty soldiers. The first and second couple immediately behind the King and Queen step out to their left and march around the castle toward their left, singing, "O, will you surrender, O, will you surrender, to the King of the Barbarees." The castle singing responds: "We won't surrender, we won't surrender, to the King of the Barbarees."

The soldiers then sing, still marching around the castle: "We'll tell the King, We'll tell the King, the King of the Barbarees."

And the castle singing replies: "You may tell the King, You may tell the King, the King of the Barbarees."

The two couples now march to the King and making him a low bow, they sing: "Good morning, good King, good morning, good King, we have a complaint to make: They won't won't surrender, they won't surrender, to the King of the Barbarees.

The King with a sweep of his right arm towards the soldiers back of him says. "Take four more of my trusty soldiers." The original couple return to the castle followed by four more soldiers from the line. They march around the castle and demand its surrender-as described above. Again they make their complaint to the King, who continues to enlarge their force until his entire resources are exhausted with the exception of the two guards standing at either side. The King now says: "Take my Queen."

The Queen marches around the castle calling upon them to surrender, but with no better result, and again they bring their complaint to the King, who says: "I will come myself then." With the two trusty guards at each side the King followed by all his soldiers, marches around the castle calling upon them to surrender, which they refuse to do. At this the King, Queen and all their followers, move off a few paces and face the castle. The soldiers line up two by two in front of the King and Queen who stand at the rear of the line, and the game proceeds by each soldier throwing himself upon the joined hands of the two children representing the castle. If he succeed in breaking down their hands he may stand back of the King, but if he fails he must stand back of the Queen. This continues until the King and Queen have each tried their strength upon the resisting castle.

The children must bear in mind that when the soldier succeeds in breaking down the hands they stand back of the King and when they lose they stand back of the Queen, and the last to try is the Queen. The score is then counted. If the number is greater on the Queen's side the Castle has won. If on the King's the King has won.

This game may finish with the two sides facing one another and having a tug of war.

DANCES AND SINGING GAMES GRADE TWO
London Town

Music: "Pop goes the Weasel." p.88

I want to go to London Town
How shall I get there?
I'll go the way the bull frog goes
That's how I'll get there!

Formation: Single circle.

Children choose an animal which they wish to imitate. All sing the song.   At the repetition of the music all move around the circle imitating the animal chosen. At the last measure the children jump up and sing lustily, "I'll never get there!" After playing airplane they sing: "We'll surely get there."

Begin with slow moving animals, gradually choosing the faster moving ones until the fastest methods of travel are reached, the automobile, the train and the airplane.

Nixie Polka
Nigarepolska
Danish

The nixie, or water sprite, comes out at certain periods during the year. Any human before whom the nixie dances receives a fairy charm, and must follow the nixie where-ever he goes.

Formation - Single circle. Face center. One in center as leader. Hands on hips.

Measures 1-4 All take four slow bleking steps, (one to each measure)- springing feet forward alternately heel on floor, toe up. On last note clap hands once.

„   5-8 Leader runs twenty-one steps to meet a partner. Others in place. Stamp twice on last measure.

Repeat, leader and partner facing. As leader turns to run to some other player,   the partner follows, placing both hands on the leader's shoulders. Repeat until all are in line.

The line may face about each time, alternating leaders. In large classes it is well   to start with two in the center, each leading his own line.

From Crampton "The Folk Dance Book" copyright 1909 by A.S. Barnes & Co. Publishers.

Nuts in May

English

Harmonized by Elizabeth Rose Fogg

1. Here we come gathering nuts in May
   Nuts in May, nuts in May,
   Here we come gathering nuts in May
   So early in the morning

2. Whom will you have for your nuts in May, etc.

3. We will have (Mary) for nuts in May, etc.

4. Whom will you have to pull her away, etc.

5. We will have (James) to pull her away, etc.

Formation: Two lines facing each other about seven feet apart.

Measures 1-4   The first line walks toward the second singing first two lines of song.
    "   5-8   Walk backward to place singing last two lines.
             Second line advances and retreats in similiar fashion to the second verse.
             The first line continues with the third, and the fifth verses after the second
             line sings the fourth verse. At the end of the fifth verse, the two players cho-
             sen (Mary and James) come out between the lines. They join right hands, and
             place one foot on a chalk mark on the floor. Each one then attempts to pull the
             other across the line. The one who loses joins the victor's line. The game is
             then repeated and is alternately started by each line.

Orange Ribbons
English

Arranged by Mabel Jenkins

1. Oh! we'll all wear orange ribbons
   orange ribbons, orange ribbons
   Oh! we'll all wear orange ribbons
   At the Ball of Primrose.

2. Oh! we'll all go gaily dancing, etc.
   At the Ball of Primrose.

Repeat second verse.

While singing the first verse walk in a stately manner, holding inside hands with partner and waving imaginary "orange ribbons" in outside hands. At the end of each verse partners face, boy bows and girl curtseys. During the repetition of the second verse, whirl with partner.

Old Roger
English

Arranged by Mabel Jenkins

1. Old Roger is dead and lies in his grave,
   Lies in his grave, lies in his grave,
   Old Roger is dead and lies in his grave
   E! I!   Lies in his grave.

2. They planted an apple tree over his head,
   Over his head, over his head,
   They planted an apple tree over his head
   E! I!   Over his head.

3. The apples were ripe and ready to drop, *etc.*

4. There came an old woman a-picking them up, *etc.*

5. Old Roger got up and gave her a thump, *etc.*

6. Which made the old woman go hippity hop, *etc.*

Formation: Circle. Choose Old Roger who lies down in center.

Verse 1. Children sing and sway from side to side as though mourning.

,, 2. Child representing apple tree enters circle, and stands at Old Roger's head with arms stretched out, and fingers spread apart.

,, 3. Tree moves arms.   Apples falling.

,, 4. Old woman comes in and picks up apples.

,, 5. Roger gets up and chases old woman, giving her a thump as indicated by the words.

,, 6. Roger lies down, and the old woman limps around the circle.

From "The North Carolina Course of Study in Physical Education." Used by permission.

Sing a Song of Sixpence

Arranged by Mabel Jenkins

Sing a song of sixpence, a pocket full of rye
Four and twenty blackbirds, baked in a pie.
When the pie was opened the birds began to sing
Wasn't that a dainty dish to set before the king!

The king was in his counting house, counting out his money,
The queen was in the pantry, eating bread and honey,
The maid was in the garden, hanging out the clothes,
And down came a blackbird and snipped off her nose!

Formation: Players in circle, facing center. Four players in center of circle crouch down, close together.

Verse I. During lines 1 and 2 circle skips to left.
During lines 3 and 4 circle stands and raises arms, and blackbirds fly a-round outside.

Verse II. During lines 1, 2, and 3 circle pantomimes counting money, eating, and hanging out clothes.
Line 4 each blackbird snips the nose of some player who becomes the blackbird when the game is repeated.

From "The North Carolina Course of Study in Physical Education." Used by permission.

On the Bridge of Avignon
Sur Le Pont D'Avignon
French

1.

(A) On the bridge of Avignon
They are passing, they are dancing;
On the bridge of Avignon
They are dancing in a ring.

(B) Gentlemen all do this way.
Then they all do this way.

2.

(B) Ladies all do this way.
Then they all do this way.

3.

(B) Soldiers all do this way.
Then they all do this way.

4.

(B) Street boys all do this way.
Then they all do this way.

Formation: Partners, single circle, hand joined.

I.

A. Measures 1 - 8 Skip around the circle to the left singing.
B.   „   9-10 Partners face, and pretending to remove their hats, make a sweeping bow
    „   11-12 Bow to neighbor.

II.

A. Measures 1 - 8 Repeat A as before.
B.   „   9-10 Repeat as in B substituting curtsey for bow.

III.

A. Measures   Repeat A as before.
B.   „   9-12 Repeat as in B substituting salute for bow.

IV.

A. Measures 1 8 Repeat A as before.
B.   „   9-12 Partners face. Put thumbs in both ears palms forward, wag like donkey ears.

A. Measures 1-8 Repeat A as before.

Swing Song

Reginald de Koven

From "Songs by Robert Louis Stevenson" Charles Scribner's Sons. Publishers. Used by permission.

How would you like to go up in a swing
Up in the air so blue?
Oh, I do think it's the pleasantest thing
Ever a child could do.
Up in the air and over the wall
Till I can see so wide,
Rivers and trees, and cattle, and all,
Over the country side.
Swinging, swinging, swinging, swinging
Over the country side.

Formation- Children in groups of three in a large circle. Two children join hands to form swing. Third child pushes swing. Those pushing swing should all be facing the same direction. At the end of the second, fourth and sixth lines the child pushing runs under swing to the next one. During the last two lines child stays at swing she has reached at 9th line.

The Roman Soldiers*

English

Arr. by Elizabeth Root

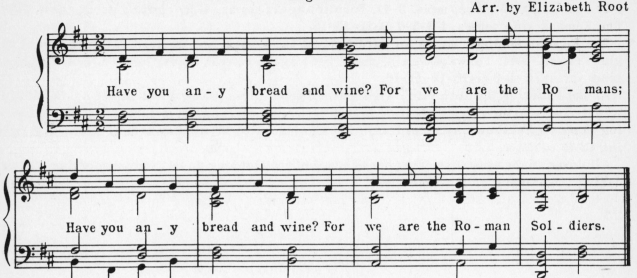

1. Have you any bread and wine?
    For we are the Romans
    Have you any bread and wine?
    For we are the Roman Soldiers.

2. Yes, we have some bread and wine
    For we are the English
    Yes, we have some bread and wine
    For we are the English Soldiers.

3. Then we will have one cup full
    For we are the Romans
    Then we will have one cup full
    For we are the Roman Soldiers.

4. No you shan't have one cup full
    For we are the English
    No you shan't have one cup full
    For we are the English Soldiers.

5. Then we will have two cups full
    For we are the Romans
    Then we will have two cups full
    For we are the Roman Soldiers.

6. No you shan't have two cups full
    For we are the English
    No you shan't have two cups full
    For we are the English Soldiers.

7. We will tell the Pope of you
    For we are the Romans
    We will tell the Pope of you
    For we are the Roman Soldiers.

8. We don't care for the Pope or you
    For we are the English
    We don't care for the Pope or you
    For we are the English Soldiers.

9. We will tell the King of you
    For we are the Romans
    We will tell the King of you
    For we are the Roman Soldiers.

10. We don't care for the King or you
    For we are the English
    We don't care for the King or you
    For we are the English soldiers.

11. We will send our cats to scratch
    For we are the Romans, etc.

12. We don't care for your cats or you
    For we are the English, etc.

13. We will send our dogs to bite
    For we are the Romans, etc.

14. We don't care for your dogs or you
    For we are the English, etc.

15. Are you ready for a fight
    For we are the Romans, etc.

16. Yes, we're ready for a fight
    For we are the English, etc.

17. Now we've only got one arm
    For we are the { Romans.
                   { English.
    Now we've only got one arm
    For we are the { Romans.
                   { English.

18. Now we've only got one leg
    For we are the { Romans.
                   { English.

19. Now we've only got one eye, etc.

From Hinman "Gymnastic and Folk Dancing" Vol. III Ring Games. Copyright 1922 by Mary Wood Hinman
A. S. Barnes & Co Publishers

Children form two straight lines facing each other. One line represents the English. One line represents the Romans. The Romans march forward toward the English line, (meas. 1-2) and repeat to place, (meas. 3-4). Forward again, (meas. 5-6) again retreat, (meas. 7-8) The Romans sing verses 1-3-5-7-9-11-13-15.

The English soldiers march forward toward the Roman line (meas. 1-2) and repeat to place (meas. 3-4). Forward again, (meas. 5-6) again retreat (meas. 7-8). The English sing verses 2-4-6-8-10-12-14-16.

At the finish of the 16th verse all shout "Shoot! Fire! Bang!" and all the soldiers drop to the floor. After a pause, all form in one big circle singing verse 17 as they march, holding their right elbows as though injured. During verse 18, all hop around circle, still holding their elbows.

All cover right eyes with right hands and continue hopping on left foot supporting elbows during the singing of the 19th verse.

The Thread Follows The Needle

From Crawford "Dramatic Games and Dances for Little Children" copyright 1914 by A.S.Barnes & Co publishers

The thread follows the needle
The thread follows the needle
In and out the needle goes
While mother mends the children's clothes.

Description: The children form in lines as in diagram I with hands joined.

Diagram I

The lines then skip forward with number 1 leading, and pass around under the arms of Nos. 10 and 9 who stand in place as in diagram (a)

Diagram a   Diagram b

Nos. 10 and 9 face in the opposite direction as the line passes under.   They are then standing with their arms crossed in front of the chest forming a chain stitch with their crossed arms. The line continues around and the next time passes between 8 and 9.(b) This continues until all the players in all the lines are turned in the opposite direction with arms all crossed in front and all sewed together. At a signal or a chord on the piano, the children turn under their arms to the right unraveling the chain, and singing at the same time R-r r-r-ip.

GRADE THREE
Bleking

From Crampton "The Folk Dance Book" copyright 1909 by A. S. Barnes & Company, Publishers.

Victor **17085**
Columbia A **3037**

Formation: Single circle, partners facing, hands joined.

Measures 1   Jump, right heel forward, right arm thrust forward, elbow straight, left arm backward, elbow bent, twist body slightly to left, weight on left foot. Jump reversing the position, left heel and arm forward, right back. Slow time.

2   Continue three times in quick succession.

(This is the Bleking step from which the dance is named.)

3 - 8   Repeat step three times.

9 - 16   Hop Waltz. Join hands and extend arms sideward. Hop left, then right, etc., turning to the right as the dance continues. Repeat from beginning.

Carrousel
Swedish
Victor 17086: Columbia A 3036

Music and description in Burchenal's "Folk Dances and Singing Games."

Hansel and Gretel Dance
German
Columbia A 3080
Humperdink

1. Partner come and dance with me   Both your hands now give to me   Right foot first   left foot then   Round and round and back a-gain   2. Tra la la la   la la la   Tra la la la   la la la,   Tra la la la   la la la la   Tra la la la   la la la.

3. With your feet go tap, tap, tap,   With your hands go clap, clap, clap,   Right foot first   left foot then Round   and round and back a-gain.

4. With your head go nip, nip, nip,   With your fin - gers snip, snip, snip,   Right foot first   left foot then Round   and round and back a-gain.

Formation: In couples scattered about the room informally or in a double circle.

Verse 1

Measures 1-4   Couples join right hands. Heel and toe polka beginning right.

      5   Place right foot forward

      6   Change weight and place left foot forward

    7-8   Drop hands and turn in place with running steps.

Verse 2

Measures 9-16   Couples join right hands and skip forward.

Verse 3

Measures 17-24 "With your feet go," all stand still.

                "Tap, tap, tap," all stamp right, left, right.

                "With your hands go," all stand still.

                "Clap, clap, clap," all clap hands.

                Right heel forward.

                Left heel forward.

                Turn in place as before.

Verse 4

Measures 17-24   repeated. Repeat, all nodding head at "nip, nip, nip," and snapping fingers at "snip, snip, snip.

I See You
Swedish

Music and description in Burchenal's "Folk Dances and singing Games."

Oh A-Hunting We Will Go
English

From Crampton & Wollaston "The Song Play Book" copyright **1917** and **1924** by A.S.Barnes & Co.,Publishers

Oh a-hunting we will go
A-hunting we will go
We'll catch a little fox
And put him in a box
And then we'll let him go.

Formation: The girls stand in one line and the boys stand opposite facing the girls. All clap their hands in time with the song, while the head couple does the following:

Measures   1 - 2   Join hands and slide down between the two lines to the foot.

          3 - 4   Slide back between lines.

          5 - 6   Drop hands, and run down outside of the lines to the foot. Repeat until every couple has been the head couple, then the two lines join hands in a ring and all dance around, repeating the verse for the last time.

For a large number of players it is advisable to have several groups of six or eight couples.

Seven Pretty Maidens in a Ring*

Sju Vackra Flickor I En Ring

Swedish

Victor 17761: Columbia A 3047

Harmonized by Elizabeth D Root

1. Seven pretty maidens in a ring
   Seven pretty maidens in a ring
   Seven pretty maidens may be seen
   In every happy circle.

2. Girls stop and turn yourselves about
   Girls stop and turn yourselves about
   See how they're turning in and out
   Within the happy circle.

3. See I will prance and you will dance
   See I will prance and you will dance
   Take now the hand I give to you
   And be my little partner.

4. Come let us dance the live long day
   Come let us dance the live long day
   Thus let us sing and dance and play
   Dancing and prancing lightly.

Girls and boys form a large ring. Seven girls join hands inside. The outer circle runs sunwise taking three steps to a measure, the inner one runs in the opposite direction. At the words "Turn yourselves" the seven girls in the inside clap their hands and face around again joining hands, still moving in the opposite direction from the outside circle. At the word "Choose" each girl selects a partner who steps into the inside circle. They stand facing one another with hands on hips, keeping time with the music by moving their heads from side to side.

At the word "Hand" clasp first right hand and then left hand. At "Now we will dance" the partners take both hands and skip around in place until the end of the music. The girl then joins the outer circle and the boy stays inside and the dance is repeated from the beginning.

*From Hinman "Gymnastic and Folk Dancing" Vol. III Ring Games. copyright 1922 by Mary Wood Hinman, A. S. Barnes & Co., Publishers..

The Sleeping Beauty

Old German

From Crawford "Dramatic Games and Dances" copyright 1914 by A.S.Barnes & Company, Publishers.

The Princess is so beautiful, beautiful, beautiful,
The Princess is so beautiful, beautiful, beautiful,

Oh, little Princess have a care, have a care, have a care,
Oh, little Princess have a care, of a wicked fay

There came a wicked fairy there, fairy there, fairy there,
There came a wicked fairy there, and said to her,

Princess! Sleep a hundred years, hundred years, hundred years,
Princess! Sleep a hundred years, and all of you.

A great hedge stood up giant high, giant high, giant high,
A great hedge stood up giant high to guard them all.

Then came a prince into this place, into this place, into this place,
Then came a prince into this place, and said to her,

Oh, little Princess, lovely maid, lovely maid lovely maid,
Oh, little Princess, lovely maid awake and arise.

The little Princess then awoke, then awoke, then awoke,
The little Princess then awoke, to be his queen.

Then was held a wedding feast, a wedding feast, a wedding feast,
Then was held a wedding feast, a wedding feast.

The people all made merry then, merry then, merry then,
The people all made merry then, through all that land.

Characters - The Princess   The Fairy
The Prince   The Courtiers
The People

Description: The Princess is in the center of a large circle pretending to spin. A small circle of children representing courtiers form around her. The other children form a large circle. The Prince and the Fairy are outside of the large circle.

Verse 1. The people move clockwise around Princess and courtiers.

2. Children stand still and lift forefinger warningly at Princess.

3. The Fairy breaks through circle and goes to Princess.

4. Princess falls down asleep and the courtiers follow her.

5. The children in the outer circle now join hand and raise them high to form a hedge.

6. The Prince breaks thru the hedge and goes to the Princess.

7. Prince sings to Princess.

8. The Prince lifts up the Princess, the courtiers awake and form in couples.

9. The Prince and the Princess walk around the circle followed by the courtiers.

10. The Prince and Princess with courtiers dance in center and those in the large circle skip about them.

Strassak

Music and description in Burchenal "Folk Dances and Singing Games."

Three Dukes
English

Music and description in Gomme and Sharp "Children's Singing Games."

Today's the First of May
English

Music and description in Burchenal "Folk Dances and Singing Games."

GRADE FOUR
Captain Jinks

I'm Captain Jinks of the horse marines,
I feed my horse on corn and beans
And swing the ladies in their 'teens,
For that's the style in the army.

I teach the ladies how to dance,
How to dance, how to dance
I teach the ladies how to dance
For that's the style in the army.

Salute your partner and turn to the right,
And swing your neighbor with all your might
And promenade with the ladies' right,
For that's the style in the army.

Formation: Double circle.

4 Measures	8 marching steps forward.
4 ,,	Hands joined with partner's. Turn partner around to left with skip.
2 ,,	Hands joined, arms sideways, 4 slides face to face.
2 ,,	Back to back with hands joined, 4 slides.
4 ,,	Repeat above 4 measures.
1 ,,	Salute partner, girls courtesy and boys bow.
1 ,,	Both turn to right.
2 ,,	Swing the one diagonally across once to left.
4 ,,	8 marching steps forward with new partner.

English Dances

The following English country dances are recommended for this grade and may be obtained at any music store for ten cents a copy or from H. W. Gray Company, New York.

New Bo-Peep, Columbia A3068.
We Won't Go Home Until Morning.

Explanation of English Folk Dance Terms

Abbreviations: r.s. running step
sk. s. skipping step
sl. s. slip step

Arm: Join elbows with partner, swing once around with four r.s. then fall back to own place with four r.s.

Cast Off: Turn outward and dance down the outside of set, then back to place thus:

Double: Four steps, either forward or backward.
Fall back: Dance backwards.
Gip: Partners dance around each other back to back, in small circle, each starting out to the left with right shoulder leading, thus:

then dance around each other face to face, each starting out to the right with left shoulder leading, thus:

Hands Across: Sets of four join either right or left hands as directions call for in wind-mill fashion, and move around circle once.

Hands All: All join hands in single circle and dance around circle.

Hands Four: Sets of four join hands and dance around in a ring clockwise.

Heys: Circular Hey: Grand right and left, without joining hands.

Whole Hey: Done by three people, 1 facing down, 2 and 3 facing up, thus:

Each individual dancer skips so as to form a figure 8, all moving at the same time, thus:

 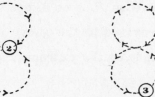

Nos 2 and 3 pass right shoulders first then 1 and 3 left shoulders. Nos 1 and 2 start on first count, but 3 waits until 3d count, around to left to face partner again on 3d and 4th steps. Return to place passing R shoulder to R shoulder, turning R to face partner on last 2 steps.

Lead: Couples join right hands and move shoulder to shoulder in same direction.

Move: Couples move forward a double without joining hands.

Half Pousette: Performed by two adjacent couples. Each couple joins both hands elbows straight. First man pushes his partner four steps out from set, then pulls her four   steps back into second couple's place. At same time second man pulls his partner four steps out of set, then pushes her four steps back into first couple's place, thus:

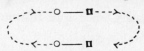

When a half pousette is followed by a repetition of the same movement, each couple de-scribing a complete circle, the figure is called the whole-pousette.

Single: (Right) A spring forward on right foot, followed by two steps in place, first with left, then with right foot. (Left) Same, springing forward on left foot.

Set: Single sideways right, followed by single sideways left.

Side: Partners face each other, pass R shoulder to R shoulder with four running steps, turning one-half way around on last two steps.

Repeat back to place passing L shoulder to L shoulder.

Slip: Slide.

Turn Single: Four running steps, turning once around in place, to the right.

Unless otherwise employed the arms always hang naturally at the sides. They are nev-er placed on the hips.

Caribou Dance

Indian

4 Caribou   Medicine Man   8 or 10 hunters

The Medicine Man enters and beats three times on a drum or tom-tom for attention, then says in a loud singing voice:

M.M.: My people, for many moons there has been no meet in our lodge and our tribe is starving. Let us call upon the Great Spirit to send success to our hunters that they may bring much caribou to save us Let us dance the Caribou Dance.

(The lines may be improvised to the above effect.)

The Medicine Man stands at the extreme right and beats his drum for the single step

M.M.: The Caribou come in

The caribou enter in single file. The left hand holding forked branches, is held at the forehead, representing horns, the right, holding a stick with strips of cloth tied to the end, representing a tail, is held at the back.

The single step is a slow prance with the knee well raised forward, a leap at each beat of the drum.

They circle the fire keeping equidistant from each other.

The Medicine Man stops beating with two quick, sharp strokes, which is always the signal for the caribou to stop dancing.

M.M.: The caribou worship the Great Mystery of Fire.

The caribou face the fire and bowing low say, "Baa-a-a."

The Medicine Man resumes his drum-beat and the caribou dance once around the fire, when the M.M. stops them with a double tap.

M.M.: The caribou worship the Four Winds of Heaven.

The caribou turn to the four points of the compass and bow saying, "Baa-a-a-a."

The Medicine Man starts to beat the double step. The caribou respond and continue the double step until the end. This is done in the same way as the single but with a slight hop on the supporting foot.

M.M.: In the fullness of the joy of life the caribou fight.

They pair off and with lowered heads and one foot advanced, they pretend to fight, with much stamping of feet and a sound made by blowing out forcibly through closed lips.

Double step around the fire.

M.M.: The caribou fight again.

As above, but changing opponents.
Drum-beat and double step around the fire.

M.M. howls like a wolf.

The caribou in a rank of four charge at the **M. M.** with the fighting action.   Drum-beat, and they dance around the fire.

M. M.:   The wolves are driven off.
Still beating, he crosses to extreme left, passing back of the caribou.   When in position he cries like a wild-cat.

The caribou attack as before.
Drum-beat and double step.

M. M.:   The hunters come in.
The hunters creep in single file until they form a semicircle back of the caribou.   The leader designates which caribou each is to shoot, then gives signal by clapping hands.
One caribou leaps high in the air and falls. The others run away.   The hunters dance in triumph around the fallen one until **M. M.** stops beating, when all sit.

M. M.: (Moves slowly into center of circle.) Behold, it never fails.   The caribou dance brings the caribou. It is great medicine. Now there is meat in the lodge.

Gustaf's Skoal
Swedish

Victor 17330

Gaily, but in the same tempo

From Crampton "The Second Folk Dance Book" copyright 1916 by A.S. Barnes & Company, publishers

The first part of the dance is slow and dignified and shows the peasants idea of the nobleman trying to enjoy himself. The second part is fast and carefree and shows the peasant really having a good time. Emphasize the mock seriouness of the first part and the abandon of the second.

Formation: In sets of four couples facing center, two head couples standing opposite and two side couples standing opposite.

Measures	1 - 2	Head couples walk three steps forward towards center and make a bobbing bow to opposite couple.
"	3 - 4	Same couples four steps backward to place.
"	5 - 8	Side couples same.
"	1 - 4	Head couples repeat.
"	5 - 8	Side couples repeat.
"	9 - 12	Side couples make arch with inside hands grasped and held high. Head couples skip forward toward center, separate and take hands of opposite, then skip through arch and around to place, meeting own partner.
"	13 - 16	All clap hands once, take both hands of partner and skip in place turning to the right, pulling away from each other.
"	9 - 16	Repeat - head couples holding arch, side couples skipping around.

Repeat from beginning.

"Skoal" means a toast or formal salute.

Indian Braves

The music for this dance will be found under "Rhythms" on page 6.

Formation: Single circle, seated on floor facing center, arms forward and elbows raised shoulder high.

Part 1

Measures	1 - 4	Bend forward and back four times.
"	5 - 8	Bend R. and L. alternately four times.
"	9 - 12	Raise arms up high with hands open, look up, fold arms. Repeat three times.
"	13 - 16	Look R. hand over eyes as if searching for something. Repeat L. R. L.
"	1 - 4 (repeated)	Listen R. with R. hand at ear, then L. with L. hand at ear. Repeat.
"	5 - 8 (repeated)	Smoke pipe four times. Pretend to hold a long pipe with bowl resting in one hand and the other hand near mouth.
"	9 - 16	Repeat listening, and smoking.

Part 2

"	17	Strike floor twice first with R and then L hand.
"	18	Give Indian Whoop 3 times.
"	19 - 20	Repeat 17 and 18.
"	21 - 24	Jump up and move around in a circle with Indian skip.
"	25 - 32	Repeat all of Part 2.

Indian Corn Husking Dance

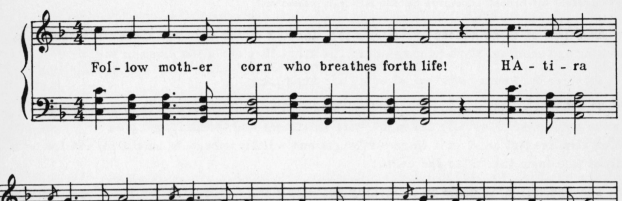

1. March around circle with corn cob in one hand.

2. Raise both hands and sing invocation.

3. Indian skip twice around circle, corn in hand.

4. Face fire. Four Indian skips in towards center. Four around self to right. Four back. Indian whoop.

5. Backs to fire; repeat 4; after "whoop" face fire.

6. Odd numbers dance four Indian skips to fire, holding up corn. Bend, offering corn to fire in four beats. Four Indian skips back.

7. Even numbers repeat this.

8. Sit, husking corn and singing. Throw husks into fire and arise.

9. Hold up corn in hand and sing entire song.

10. March around circle once and exit.

Corn is spoken of as Atira (mother) with prefix H signifying breath, the sign of life.

Hopi Corn Dances
Indian

The first of these dances symbolizes the planting of the corn and the second its gathering husking and shelling. Each is complete in itself but they are often given in sequence.

The "grain of corn" and "ear of corn" are imaginary.

The "sun and shimmer sign" indicates the sunshine pouring down. It is made by holding up the outside hand, usually the right, with forefinger and thumb forming an "O"; at the same time the left hand with fingers straight and a little spread, is moved to and fro in a direct line from the "O" to the earth.

The "rain sign" is made by stretching both arms out straight, palms down and moving the fingers up and down in time to the music.

The "hop step" is the principle step. It consists of a hop and a step on each foot. The hop is very slight so that at times only the heel leaves the floor. The knees are turned out and slightly bent. The knee action is emphatic, causing a vibration and jingle of the rattles which are often attached to the leg.

The "side step" is done in slow rhythm. Take long step to the side with the right foot on the heavy beat of the drum. Slide left foot up to right on the light beat of the drum.

The "wind murmur" is a continuous soft sound made by prolonging "oo" in unison and softly rising and falling a little in intensity. The usual accompaniment is the beat of a drum. "Fire" means the center of the circle.

The Spring Dance
or
The Planting of the Corn

Tribal Prayer

Harmonized by
Prof. J. C. Fillmore

Translation:
  Father a needy one stands before thee;
  I that sing am he.

Rain Song

Tigua

Transcribed and Harmonized
By Prof. J. C. Fillmore

Hla-chi dai - nin, hla-chi dai - nin, i - beh ma kun whi ni weh, da win gu ba hin ah.
Rain Rain Rain People, Rain Rain Rain People Rain up-on our plain people, Rain Rain   Rain Rain

1. Walk in, one behind the other, to the beating of a drum, raising knee high at each step, holding corn in both palms, at face level. Continue round the fire until equal distances apart.

2. Put corn into right palm; raise left hand, palm forward, and sing the "Tribal Prayer."

3. Down on right knee (3 counts) dig hole with right forefinger (3 counts), put grain of corn into hole (1 count). Cover with two movements, and pat (4 counts) rise (4 counts).

4. Side step to left, shading eyes with hands, till each is in position at opposite side of circle from starting point (8 counts).

5. Four steps in towards fire (4 counds).

6. Spread hands over fire (4 counts); rub it into body (4 counts); spread hands over fire (4 counts); rub it in (4 counts).

7. Back out 4 steps (4 counts).

8. Rain Song, with rain sign.

9. Hop step, making shimmer sign, 1½ times around the ring, bringing each back to original position.

10. Kneel (4 counts), left hand on left knee, put back of right hand on the ground with fingers closed except index which points up, raise it in 4 jerks to 4 counts, to make the corn grow knee high.

11. Same as 5.

12. Same as 6.

13. Same as 7.

14. Same as 8.

15. Same as 9, going once round fire.

16. Kneel (4 counts), left hand extended a little to lower left side, making corn grow to waist level.

17. Repeat 5, 6, 7, 8, 9.

18. Bend body a little forward at waist (4 counts) make corn grow to head level (4 counts)

19. Repeat 5, 6, 7, 8, 9.

20. The hands high, waving corn, sway forward, backward, left and right, forward, backward, left and right, giving 2 counts to each, uttering wind murmur.

21. Four side steps to left, turn to left, war-whoop with right hand, holding left as if warding off enemy. Do this 4 times.

22. With head bent downward on folded arms in sign of night, glide off after leader.

The Fall Dance
or
The Husking of the Corn

1. Enter marching, holding up corn-cob in one hand. Form complete circle facing fire.

2. Stop, raise both hands, and sing the "Tribal Prayer."

3. Hop-step around twice, corn in hand.

4. Face fire, four steps in, turn in place with four steps, and four steps back. (Indian Whoop.)

5. Backs to fire repeat 4; after Indian Whoop face fire.

6. Odd numbers dance four steps to fire, holding up corn. Bend, offering corn in four beats four steps back.

7. Even numbers repeat 6.

8. Sit, husking the corn to song of chekah boy tehik (bark canoe). Then shell corn to same song. Throw husks into fire and rise.

9. Hold corn in hands and sing Wah! Taho! Go once around in march step and march out.

Note: For the Fall Dance use the "Corn Grinding Song", p.1, "Songs of Ancient America" by Natalie Curtis, published by G. Schirmer, New York, or the Zuni Sunrise Call, Carlos Troyer.

Minuet
French
Beethoven

The Minuet was brought to Paris in 1650 from the outlying districts. It was at first gay and lively but when brought to court it lost its sportive character and became very dignified due to the formal costumes, enormous head dresses, tight waists and hugh skirts.Pointing the toe enabled the ladies to show their pointed slippers and tiny feet, and the gentlemen to show their buckles and silk stockings. During the reign of Louis XV, it was danced extensively. It is the perfect expression of an age in which courtesy, ceremony and chivalry were brilliantly polished. The fact that the minuet measure has been incorporated into the structure of the symphony shows how important a part it played in the world.

Formation: Double circle, facing counter clockwise; inside hands joined, boy on left, or inside, girl on right.

A

Measure 1 Step inside, outside, inside.

   ,,   2 Point outside. (2 counts.) Step outside.

   ,,   3 Point inside (2 counts) Step inside.

   ,,   4 Point outside (3 counts)

   ,,   5 Step outside, inside, outside.

   ,,   6 Point inside (3 counts).

   ,,   7 Make a small circle turning away from partner stepping inside, outside, inside.

   ,,   8 Facing partner, step sideward in line of direction and bow.

A (repeated)

   ,,   1-8 Repeat all of A.

B

Measure 1 Partners join right hands and change places stepping inside, outside, inside.

   ,,   2 Point outside (3 counts)

   ,,   3 Return to places stepping outside, inside, outside.

   ,,   4 Again face forward and point inside (3 counts)

   ,,   5-8 Repeat A measures 1-4.

B (repeated)

   ,,   1-4 Repeat as above starting with outside foot.

   ,,   5-8 Repeat as above substituting a step and bow instead of step and point of measure 8.

Money Musk
American

Formation: Double line, partners facing.

Four couples in a set.

Measures 1 - 4   Head couple join hands. Swing once and a half around.

"   5 - 8   First girl steps between second and third boy. First boy steps between second and third girl. All balance forward and back, twice.

"   1 - 4   Each group of three swings around in place.

(repeated)

"   5 - 8   All balance forward and back, twice, as before.

(repeated)

"   9 - 12   Same as first four measures.

"   13 - 16   First girl steps between third and fourth boy. First boy steps between third and fourth girl. All balance, as before.

"   9 - 12   Same as repeat of Measures 1 - 4.

(repeated)

"   13 - 16   Head couple casts off (run). All promenade following head couple. This figure leaves the head couple at the foot and the second couple at the head. Repeat until all are in original places.

Norwegian Mountain March

Music and description in Burchenal's "Folk Dances and Singing Games."

Pop Goes the Weasel
American

Victor **17160**
Columbia **A3078**
Edison **50749**

Formation: Double line, partners facing, four couples in a set.

Measures 1 - 8   Head couple leads down the center and returns to place.

   "   **1 - 8**   Head couple casts off, skips down outside of lines, meets at bottom of
(repeated)   set, returns to place between lines.

   "   **9 - 10**   Head couple balances with second girl.

   "   **11 - 14**   Three hands around with second girl.

   "   **15 - 16**   Second girl returns to place under arms of head couple.   This leaves
the head couple facing second boy.   Repeat measures **9 - 16** with
second boy, and so on down the set, zig-zagging across, thus: second girl, second boy, third girl, third boy, etc.

When all have been "popped" head couple casts off and all promenade,
following head couple. This figure brings the second couple at the
head with the first head couple at the foot.

Seven Jumps
SYVSPRING
Danish

Victor **17777**

Seven Jumps is a very vigorous dance and in Denmark is usually performed only by men, very often with a leader standing in the center of the circle. The men are very particular that no one move during the second part of the dance and anyone discovered so doing must buy refreshments for the rest of the group.

Formation: Single circle with a leader in the center if so desired.

Measures:

I. A. **1 - 8** With hands joined all skip to the left (one skip to a measure.)

   B. **9 - 16** Jump up high and repeat the skip moving to the right.

   C. **17** Release hands, place them on hips, and **raise right foot from ground,** knee bent at right angles.

     18 Replace foot and remain motionless.

II.   **1 - 16** Repeat all.

    17-18 Same as before.

    17-18 Raise left leg and replace.
  (repeated)

III. **1 18**⎫
    17-18⎬ Repeat All.
  (repeated)

    17-18 Kneel on right knee. Remain until first note of measure **1** is played.
  (repeated)

Continue repeating A and B. Each time add one extra repeat of measures **17** and **18** and add the following movements to those already performed in C:

Kneel on left knee (all are now down on both knees)

Place **right** elbow on floor, chin resting on right hand.

Place left elbow on floor, chin resting on both hands.

Place forehead on floor.

Finish dance with A and B.

Vineyard Dance

French

Sprightly

Measures 1 - 8   March in and form circle. Face center.

9 - 16   Make motion of digging and patting the ground. Tap three times with feet right, left, right, placing hands on hips. Repeat three times. The last time turn around to the right while tapping. These movements are intended to call out the spirits of the earth to make the vines grow.

9 - 16   Make motion of gathering grapes and placing them in baskets. Tap feet as before, thanking the spirits for the bountiful harvest. Form double circle facing clockwise.

17 - 24   Skip around circle with partner.

25 - 32   Face partners. Four steps forward to partner's place, passing to the right, turn, bow (4 counts) Repeat, returning to place.

GRADE FIVE
Buck and Wing*

*From Hinman "Gymnastic and Folk Dances" Vol. V Clogs and Jigs. copyright by Mary Wood Hinman,
A.S. Barnes & Co., publishers.

I. Sixteen three's, 8 measures.

II. Forward fall out on L foot, back on R foot, 8 measures.
Three 3's.
Forward fall out on R foot, back on L foot.
Three 3's.
Repeat.

III. 1. Brush left foot forward and back   8 measures.
2. Step L foot behind R foot, R foot to side, step L foot in front.
3. Brush R foot forward and back.
4. Repeat (2) to R.

IV. 3-3-7, 8 measures.
Repeat

V. Wing to side (Walk three steps forward starting L foot, placing R heel to L toe etc.,
toes turned out.)
3 jumps forward, backward, forward, (heels together.)
Three 3's left right, left.
Half turn right, draw semi-circle with R toe, finish heels together.
Repeat all.

VI. Jump forward, backward, forward to deep knee. 4 counts. Rise, turn left about on right
foot (left knee raised) forward left, four 3's. Repeat.

VII. Hands on hips, hop on right foot, swing left forward. Count 1.
Hop right, swing left foot back to right knee. Count 2.
Repeat through seven counts.
Repeat all starting on opposite foot.

VIII. Arms folded- Repeat all changing on 4th count. In place of last change slap back
right. Arms sideward.

IX. Step right back 3's left and right.
Tap left, step left.
Brush right forward and hop left.
Slap back right.
Repeat 3 times, last time finish with brush forward.

Bow 1. Bend forward, right leg raised backward, arms side.
2. Stand in errect position.

Country Dance

Music and description in Frost, "Clog and Character Dances."

Csebogar

Pronounced Che´-bo-gar
Hungarian

Victor 17821

Formation: Partner dance, single circle, hands joined.

Measures 1 - 4 Eight slides to the left.
    ,,   5 - 8 ,,   ,,   ,, ,, right.
    ,,   1 - 2 Four skips toward center of circle.
    ,,   3 - 4 ,,   ,, back to place.
    ,,   5 - 8 Hungarian turn.

           Partners face one another. Place right arm around waist of partner.
           Raise left arm above head. Hop right, step left, step right. Repeat three
           times, doing step four times in all.
           Partners face one another single circle. Boy places hands on girls waist.
           Girl places hands on boys' shoulders and in this position.

    ,,   9 - 12 Four draws toward center of circle.
    ,, 13 - 16 ,,   ,, back to place.
    ,,   9 - 10 Two   ,, towards center
    ,, 11 - 12 ,,   ,, back to place
    ,, 13 - 16 Hungarian turn. Finish with a shout.

Dutch Couples

Arr. by Fannie Robertson

Andante

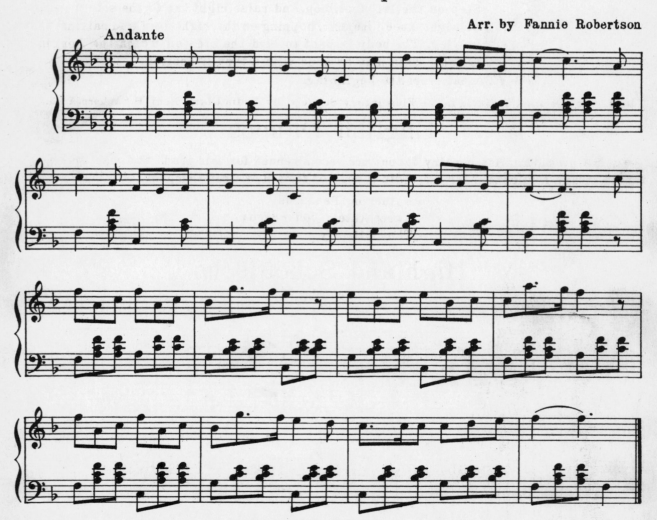

Formation: Double circle facing right.

I. Measures 1   Dutch step forward as follows: Step to side with slight stamp of the left foot, brush the right forward, and click the heel on the floor, using a count for each step.

,,   2 - 4 Repeat above.

II. Measures 5   Place hands on hip. Turn away from partner, take six short running steps in a small circle, and face partner.

,,   6   Bend forward, arms raised at sides to shoulder level. Raise trunk and sink arms to sides, knees stiff.

,,   7 - 8 Repeat running and bowing.

III. Measures 9-10 Hands at hips. Step back on the left foot, hop, and swing the right foot forward. Repeat, stepping back on the right foot. Repeat, left and right.

,,   11-12 Repeat, going forward.

,,   13-16 Dutch waltz (eight steps.) Join hands, arms raised to shoulder level. Step on the left foot; hop, and raise right leg to the side   with straight knee. Repeat, hopping on the right foot and raising the left leg. The body is bent toward the side on which the hopping is done. This may be done with a turn if desired.

Repeat from the beginning.

Taken from "Physical Training in the Elementary Schools" by Lydia Clark. Benj. H. Sanborn & Co., Publishers.

English Dances

The following English country dances are recommended for this grade and may be obtained at any music store for ten cents a copy or from H. W. Gray Company, New York.

> Gathering Peascods
> Sweet Kate - Victor 18004
> The Butterfly

Highland Schottische
Scotch

Victor 17331
Columbia A 3039

Formation: Single circle. Partners face each other. Left arm raised over head, right hand on hip.

Measures 1 - 4 (1) Touch right toe to right side, hop left. (2) Raise right in back of left knee, hop left. (3) Touch right toe to right side, hop left. (4) Raise right in front of left knee, hop left. (5 - 8) Schottische step to right- step together, step hop. Repeat step starting to left, right arm up.

5 - 12 Partners hook right arms, left hands on hips. Four schottische steps turning partner. Repeat twice. On the last measure run forward four steps past your own partner to meet new partner.

Repeat from beginning.

How Do You Do

Order I, II, I, II, I.
1 2 3 4 5

Formation: Two by two, in couples forming a circle around the room. Every other couple about face, to make a formation of fours facing.

Measures 1 - 8 I. With hand joined each couple takes three slides to left, and heels together.

Repeat back to place (four measures)

Four hands round   ,,   ,,

,, 9 - 16 II. Forward and back (four measures)

Forward and stop two   ,,

Join right hands with opposite, count (1) make a downward movement (shake hands, How do you do?), count (2) join left hands still keeping right hands joined, count (3) make downward movement, count (4) two measures. As the hands are joined and the downward movement is made, the dancers should say "How do you do?" keeping time to the four movements.

,, 1 - 8 III. All take seven slides to center of room, and heels together.

All slide back to places.

,, 9 - 16 IV. Give right hands across to diagonal and go once around; give left hands across and go once around in opposite direction.

,, 1 - 8 V. Forward and back. Forward and pass through opposite couple, each person going to her own right. Forward and curtsey to new couple.

Repeat from the beginning with new couple.

Káčă

Pronounced Ka ćha

Czecho Slovakian

Arranged by Jan Schuster

From Geary "Folk Dances of Czecho Slovakia" copyright 1922 by A.S. Barnes & Company, publishers.

Formation: Couples. Double circle, facing forward, girl in the outside circle.

The music is divided into two parts, A of twelve measures and B of eight. In fitting the steps to the music each measure should be counted "one, two, three."

A

Partners face and grasp inside hands, raising the arms backward above the shoulder level.

Measures 1   Step forward on the outside foot (one), close with the inside foot (two), step forward on the outside foot (three). During this movement swing the arms forward and turn back to back with partner.

,,   2   Repeat measure **1** beginning with the inside foot. This step must be taken in place, turning towards partner and swinging the arms backwards.

,,   3 - 12 Repeat measures **1 - 2** five times.

B

,,   1 - 8 Partners drop hands, the boy steps around in front, facing partner and both give right hands. With **24** running steps all make a grand chain (grand right and left) girls moving around the circle from left to right, boys in the opposite direction.

The dance is usually repeated several times, each time with a new partner met at the end of the dance.

Knytnapspolska

Danish

Victor 17963

Formation: In couples, facing partners; both hands joined and pulling back away from partners.

Step. The Polska step is executed thus: begin left, slide twice to left (slide, close, slide) and leap on to right foot across in front of left foot. This step is also done beginning right foot and leaping on to left.

Measures 1 - 3	Begin left, three polska steps to left, couples making a small circle in place.
4	Stamp left, stamp right, stamp left.
1 - 3	Three polska steps to right.
4	Stamp right, stamp left, stamp right.
5	Both jump and land on both feet, turning so that right elbow points toward partner. Hands on hips.
6	Jump again, facing so that left elbow points towards partner.
7	Repeat measure 5 this time shake clenched fist at partner.
8	Repeat measure 6 and shake left fist at partner.
9-10	Join hands with partner and whirl in place, pivoting on right foot. End with a stamp of left foot on last count.

Sellenger's Round*

or

"The Beginning of the World"

English

Victor 18018
Columbia A 3065

Harmonized by Elizabeth Root

Among the dances popular in Queen Elizabeth's time was a dance called "Sellenger" or "Sillinger" and the tune is thought to be one of the oldest now in existence. It is mentioned by Taylor in his book called "The World Runs on Wheels" as "The Beginning of the World". There is a description of this old dance in Playford. It reads as follows:

"The dancers take hands, and go around twice and back again; then all set, turn and repeat; then lead all forward and back, and repeat; two singles and back, set and turn single, and repeat; sides all, and repeat; arms all, and repeat; danced as often in circles as in parallel lines". It is also included in many May Day customs, and is said to date back to 1450. It seems to have been the favorite tune to which the villagers danced about their Maypole.

* *From* Hinman "Gymnastic and Folk Dancing" Vol. III Ring Games. Copyright 1922 by Mary Wood Hinman
A. S. Barnes & Co. Publishers.

Part I

Measures 1 - 8 Hands all, eight slips clockwise and eight slips counter clockwise to
                 places.
  ,,   9 - 10 All move forward two singles toward the center.
  ,,   11 - 12 All fall back a double to places.
  ,,   13 - 16 Partners set and turn single.
  ,,   9 - 16 All that again.
  (repeated)

Part II

Measures 1 - 4 All take hands, move forward a double to the center, and fall back
                 a double to places.
  ,,   5 - 8 That again.
  ,,   9 - 16 As in first part.
  ,,   9 - 16
  (repeated)

Part III

Measures 1 - 4 Partners side.
  ,,   5 - 8 That again.
  ,,   9 - 16 As in first part.
  ,,   9 - 16
  (repeated)

Part IV

Measures 1 - 4 Partners arm with the right.
  ,,   5 - 8 Partners arm with the left.
  ,,   9 - 16 As in first part.
  (repeated)

*From Hinman's "Gymnastic and Folk Dances", Vol. III Ring Games, Copyright 1922 by Mary Wood Hinman,
A. S. Barnes & Co. Publishers

School Boy Antics

For Boys

Music and description in Frost's "Clog Dance Book."

Skobodansen
(Pronounced Skoó-bo-dan-sen)
Swedish

For Boys

In Sweden this peculiarly dramatic dance is performed only by men. In 1885 this dance was performed by old farmers at a Christmas festival in Hofterup, County of Harjagers, Province of Skane.

Music: **1-16 ‖ 17-32 ‖** The first part of the music is played in a very slow tempo even slower than the old waltz; the second part is considerably faster.

Formation: Partners facing, either in a line or a circle.

I

Measure **1**   Partners A and B, join both hands and with three ordinary walking steps move around sunwise in a small circle,   beginning with the left foot.

”   **2**   Stamp right, pause.

”   **3 - 8**   Repeat above, continuing to move in the same direction.

”   **9 - 16**   Repeat all, moving contra-sunwise, beginning with the right foot and stamping with the left.

The entire first part has a hesitating, slow, dignified character in contrast to second part which is dramatic and aggressive.

II

Measure **17**   A and B drop hands. Make complete turn sunwise with three steps.

”   **18**   A bends quickly. B circles left leg out and then over A's head.

”   **19**   Both turn completely around as in measure 17.

”   **20**   A kicks over B's head.

”   **21**   Both turn completely around as in measure 17.

”   **22**   Bend forward towards each other so that foreheads touch.

”   **23**   Keeping heads together, both turn and finish back to back.

”   **24**   With a vigorous movement of the body, each pushes the other away.

”   **25-32**   Repeat above.

Three Dance
Tretur
Danish

The music consist of three parts A, B, and C and is played once through (with repeats) as written for each figure.

Formation: Four couples in quadrille formation. 1st and 2nd couples standing opposite each other (head couples) and second and third couples opposite each other (side couples) Free hands always on hips.

"Circle"

A Measure 1 - 8   All eight dancers join hands and dance around in a circle to the left, as follows: Step lf; hop lf; step rt; hop rt.

A Measure 1 - 8   Repeat same in opposite direction. Spread circle to its fullest extent by leaning backward away from the center. The steps should be brisk so that the swing of the circle is vigorous.

"Back to Back"

B Measure 9-12   Start with right foot. Couples 1 and 2 move forward with 8 running steps, couple 2 separates allowing couple 1 to pass between them.

Measure 13-16   Without turning around, both couples run eight short steps backward to places. This time couple 1 separates and couple 2 passes between them.

B Measure 9-16   Couples 3 and 4 repeat same, couple 3 passing inside going over and separating as they return to place.

"Clap and Swing"

Use same step as in "Circle"

C Measure 17-18   Head couples move toward each other at the same time clapping hands 3 times.

Measure 19-20   Each boy and opposite girl hook right arms and swing once around (lf hands on hips.)

Measure 21-24   Partners hook lf. elbows and swing once around, finishing in original position. In swinging with hooked elbows the dancers should pull away from each other and swing vigorously.

Measure 25-32   The side couples repeat the same.

Repeat entire dance.

GRADE SIX
Clogs

In addition to the clogs printed for this grade, the following are recommended. Descriptions and music for these dances are in Frost "The Clog Dance Book."

Captain Jinks
There Was An Old Man
Yankee Doodle

Rig-a-Jig (In Frost "Clog and
              Character Dances")

Janko
John
Czecho Slovakian

Arranged by K. Kovarovic

From Geary "Folk Dances of Czecho Slovakia", copyright 1922 by A.S. Barnes & Co., publishers

The music consists of two parts, A of eight measures and B, which is repeated, making sixteen measures. In fitting the steps to the music each measure should be counted: "one, two."

Formation: Partners, double circle, facing forward, girl in outside circle.

A

Boy places right arm around girl's waist; she places inside hand on his right shoulder. Outside hands on hips.

Measures 1 - 8 Balance forward on the left and back on the right foot, eight times. The body should be bent slightly backward and forward and the head turned alternately towards and away from partner.

1 B

Measures 1 - 6 Partners keep the same position as in A. With twelve little running steps, beginning with the outside foot, make a complete turn right, the boy running in place while swinging the girl backward.

,,   7 Partners place hands on hips and with a quarter turn jump, landing on both feet, partners face (one,) stamp right (two.)

,,   8 Stamp left (one), stamp right (two).

2 B

,,   1 - 6 Repeat 1B, measures 1 - 6, boy placing left arm around partner's waist and both turning left.

,,   7 - 8 Boy throws the girl from his left to his right arm while she makes a complete turn right with three short leaping steps. Partners are now in their original positions ready to repeat the dance.

Jumping - Jack's Jubilee*

For Boys

*From Hinman "Gymnastic & Folk Dancing" copyright by Mary Wood Hinman, A.S. Barnes & Co., publishers

STEP 1

Measure 1	Slide right foot obliquely forward, raising left leg backward. Left hand
Count 1	obliquely backward, downward. Right hand upward.
Count 4	Hop on right foot, raising left leg backward. Right hand obliquely forward, upward. Left hand obliquely backward, downward.
Measure 2	Slide left foot obliquely forward, raising left leg backward, and change
Count 1	arm positions.
Count 4	Hop on left foot, raising right leg backward. Arms as above.
Measure 3	
Count 1	Slide right foot obliquely forward, arms as above.
Count 4	Hop on right foot, arms same as in Meas. 1.
Measure 4	
Count 1	Hop on right foot, arms same as in Meas. 1.
Count 4	Hop on right foot, arms same as in Meas. 1.
Measure 5	Step backward on to left foot raising right across left leg, right knee
Count 1	bent. Right arm circled across body, left arm overhead.
Count 4	Hop on left foot, arms remain the same.
Measure 6	Step backward on to right foot raising left across right leg, left knee
Count 1	bent, left arm across body, right arm circled upward.
Count 4	Hop on right foot, arms remain the same.
Measure 7	Hop backward on to left foot, raising right across left leg, arms circled
Count 1	at front horizontal.
Count 4	Hop backward on to right, raising left across right leg, arms same.
Measure 8	Repeat measure 7.
Count 1 - 4	
Measure 9 - 16	Repeat whole step, beginning left.

STEP 2

Measure 17	Cross right over left.
Count 1 - 3 - 5	Slide right foot across left, bend left knee and body sideways, left arm sideways and step left foot sideways.
	Close right foot to left foot, and slide left foot sideways left.
Measure 18	
Count 1	Slide left foot across right and step right foot sideways.
Count 1 - 3 - 5	Close left foot to right foot and slide right foot sideways right.

(The three movements are made in two movements.)

Measure 19-20   Repeat action of measures 17 and 18.
Count   1-3-5

Measure 21   Slide right foot obliquely forward, raising left leg well backward, right
Count   1   arm obliquely forward upward, left arm downward.
Count   4   Hop on right foot.

Measure 22   Step backward on left foot, raise right leg forward, left-arm upward,
Count   1   right hand on hip.
Count   4   Hop on left foot.

Measure 23-24   Four hops on right foot, $\frac{1}{4}$ turn to right on each hop right arm upward,
Count 1-4 1-4   left hand on hip.
                 Repeat, starting with left, using measures 25-32.

STEP 3

Measure 33   "Two-step sideways"
Count   1   Slide right foot to right, left arm upward, right hand on hip and bring
                     left foot to right foot.
Count   4   Hop on left foot raising right foot upward.
                 (Three movements in two counts.)

Measure 34   Repeat Measure 33.
Count   1-4

Measure 35   3 hops on right foot with $\frac{1}{4}$ turn right on each hop. Right arm upward,
Count   1-4   left hand on hip.

Measure 36
Count   1 hold   Repeat to left measures 37-40
                 Repeat whole step, measures 41-48.

STEP 4

Measure 49   "The Cobbler" or "Scissors"
Count   1   Jump to side, straddle on heels, arms obliquely sideways upward.
Count   3   Jump to squat, hands on hips.
Count   4   Jump to side, straddle on heels.
Count   6   Jump to squat, hands on hips.

                 Measures 50 to 56 repeat action of measure 49.
Measure 57   Straighten knees, raise right leg sideways.
Count   1   Hop on left foot and describe circle with right foot. ("Twist" or vokes.)

Measure 58
Count   1   Touch right toe behind left heel. Hop on left foot.
Count   4   Kick right leg sideways. Hop on left foot.

Measure 59
Count   1   Step on right foot and raise leg sideways, left
Count   4   Hop on right foot and "twist" left leg.

Measure 60   Hop on right foot and touch left toe behind right heel.
Count   1   Hop on right foot and raise left leg sideways left.
Count   4   Repeat action for 57 to 60 using measure 61 to 64.

STEP 5

Measure 1   "The Rock"(Rubber legs)
Count   1   Swing left foot in front of right,raising right heel. Hands clasped in front.
Count   4   Lower right heel and raise left heel.

Measure 1-8   Repeat above action.

Measure 9   Weight on left foot, raise right leg sideways right.
Count   1   Twist right leg (vokes)
Count   4

Measure 10   Weight on right foot, raise left leg sideways left.
Count   1   Twist left leg. (vokes)
Count   4

Measure 11-12 Repeat action for meas. 9-10.
Count   1-4

Measure 13-14 Four hops on left foot.
Count   1-4

Measure 15-16 3 hops to right on right $\frac{1}{4}$ turn on each hop, right arm upward   left
Count   1-4   hand on hip.
Count   1 hold

STEP 6

Measure 17   "The Mandarin"
Count   1   Hop on left foot, bend left knee. Place right heel obliquely forward right.
                   Right arm obliquely sideways upward, left arm downward.
Count   2   Reverse positions of hands and feet.

Measure 18-20 Repeat above action.

Measure 21-22 Slide right foot obliquely forward, right arm obliquely forward upward
Count   1-4   left arm downward.
Count   1-4   Three hops on right foot.

Measure 23-24 4 hops on left foot $\frac{1}{4}$ turn left, on each hop, left arm upward, right hand
Count   1-4 1-4   on hip.

Measure 25-32 Repeat, starting with left foot use action of meas. 17-24.

STEP 7

Measure 33   "The Cartwheel"
Count   1   Weight on left foot, raise right foot sideways right.
Count   4   "Twist" right leg.

Measure 34

Count   1   Weight on right foot, raise left leg sideways left.

Count   4   "Twist" left leg.

Measure 35-36 "Cartwheel" to L. or step on L. complete turn to L.

Measure 37-40 Repeat other side, right.

Measure 41-48 Repeat entire step.

STEP 8

"Handspring."

Measure 49-53 Same as in first step, only begin with L. foot.

Measure 53   Step left foot sideways turning instep to floor, both knees bent.
              (grotesque as "Break leg")

Measure 54   Reverse of meas. 53.

Measure 55-56 Repeat action for meas. 53-54 only change weight 3 times.

Measure 57-60 Repeat action for meas. 49-53 starting with left foot.

Measure 61-62 Walk backward 3 steps beginning left.

Measure 63-64 Walk forward 2 steps and handspring forward or sit on ground.

Kerry Dance
Irish

Oh, the days of the Kerry dancing!
Oh, the ring of the piper's tune
Oh for one of those hours of gladness!
Gone alas! like our youth, too soon.
When the boys begin to gather
In the glen in the summer night
And the Kerry piper's tuning
Made us long with wild delight.
Oh, to think of it! Oh, to dream of it!
Fills my heart with tears.
Oh, the days of the Kerry dancing!
Oh, the ring of the piper's tune,
Oh, for one of those hours of gladness!
Gone alas! like our youth, too soon.

Formation - Double line, partners facing. The dance is started by the two top couples, all the others awaiting their turn.

I BALANCE. _ 4 measures

> Gentleman of leading couple and lady of second couple face each other, and similarly the lady of leading couple and gentleman of second couple balance to time in place. (Forward and back, twice.)

II RIGHT HANDS ACROSS. _ 4 measures

> Gentleman of leading couple gives right hand to right hand of lady of second couple, similarly lady of leading couple and gentleman of second couple, all dance full round to left. (Springy walking steps) Release hands.

III BALANCE.- As in I _ 4 measures

IV LEFT HANDS ACROSS. _ 4 measures

> As in II giving left hands instead of right.

V ADVANCE DOWN CENTER. _ _ _ _ _ _ _ _ _ _ _ _ _ _ _ _ _ 4 measures

> Leading couple face down set, join inside hands, and advance. _ _ _ _ 4 measures
> Release hands, turn about, join inside hands and return to place. _ _ _ 4 measures

VI DANCE ROUND. _ 2 measures

> Gentleman of leading couple passes round at back of gentleman of second   6 measures
> couple. His partner at the same time passes round at back of lady of
> **second couple,** and each meet the other below the second couple.

> Gentlemen of leading and second couples take own partners both hands,
> Two couples dance round each other in circle, second couple finishing up
> at head of line and leading couple coming to rest in place vacated by second
> couple.

The leading couple and third couple now dance together, (second couple resting,) the same movements being repeated. The third couple finish up in place vacated by leading couple coming to rest in place vacated by third couple. Leading couple then dance with fourth couple and second and third couples dance together. The movement is thus continued until all are dancing, the couples changing places each time. The dance is generally concluded when the leading couple have returned to their original position.

From "A Handbook of Irish Dances" by O'Keefe and O'Brein.

Little Man in a Fix
Bitte Mand I Knibe
Danish

Victor 18552

Music ‖: 1-8 :‖: 9-16 :‖
Danced by two couples

Measures 1 - 8 (a) **Boys hook their left arms and run contra-sunwise, clasping girls' waists with their right. Girls rest their left hands on boys' left shoulders. The more the girls are swung, the more they must lean back.**

        (b) **Without stopping, gentlemen seize each other's left hands, and swinging girls in front of them, raise their left arms to allow ladies to run through arch. The boys turn contra-sunwise and seize each other's right hands over boys' and continuing, all four run contra-sunwise, with arms crossed and facing toward center.**

  "   9 - 16 (c) **Waltz with own partner.**

  "   9 - 16   **Repeat dance several times.**

Oxdansen
Swedish

For Boys

Music and description in Crampton's "The Folk Dance Book"

Reap The Flax
Swedish

Music and description in Crampton's "The Folk Dance Book"

Tinker's Dance
Kedelflikkerdans
Danish

Victor **17962**

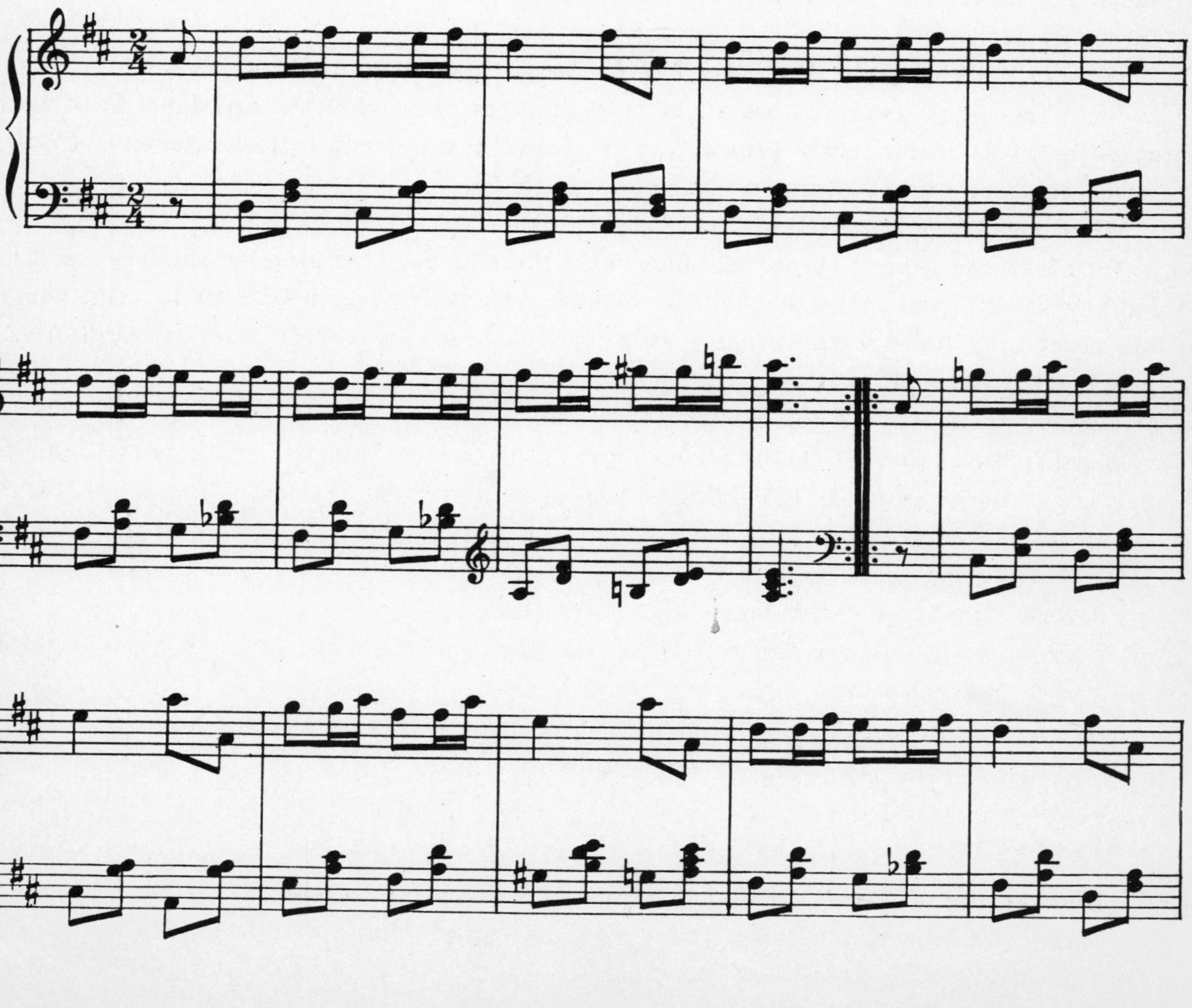

Music: ‖: 1-8 :‖: 9-16 :‖: 17-24 :‖

One gentleman and two ladies. First three with back to front, second three opposite them, facing front, third and other threes behind second three, also facing front. As many threes as desired.

Steps: Tinker's step, **The Other Night's Step**, skip step, walking step.

(a) First gentleman and his right lady turn toward each other and dance four tinker's steps in place inside hands joined. (1-4), then dance round in place, turning to the left, with the other night's steps, waist position (5-8).

Gentleman repeats with his left lady (1-8).

(b) First and second threes advance with three steps, stamping on the first, make a little bow (9-10) and retire backwards (11-12). First gentleman lifts both arms, whereupon his right lady turns with skipping steps twice around to the left under his right arm, still holding his hand (13-16).

Repeat with lady on left making the turn.

(c) First and second threes form separate circle, clasping the upper part of each other's arms, and dance sunwise (17-20) and contra-sunwise (21-24) with skip steps. The first three moves round to the left, until in the place of the second three, who gain the place of first three in the same manner (17-24).

Second time first three dance with third three.

Third time first three dance with fourth three, second with third, a new couple beginning every second time.

After having danced through the row, first three turns round, so as to face front, and waits until next three comes up ready to dance.

If many participate, every fourth three may take position like first three and begin at the same time.

Description of steps: Tinker's Step; this is similiar to a setting step. At the break the rear foot describes a small circle as it is brought forward. Other Night's Step: a step-hop turn backwards instead of forward.

Sicilian Circle
American

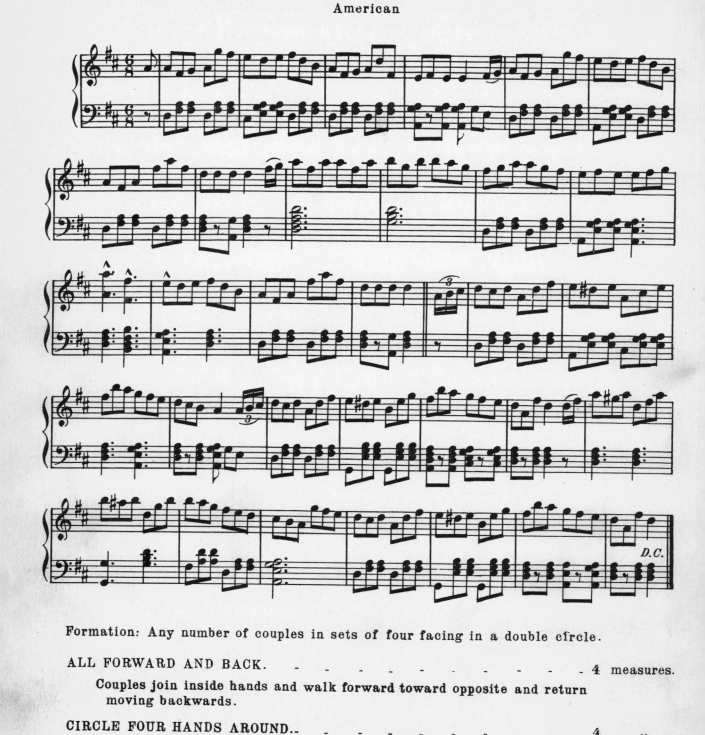

Formation: Any number of couples in sets of four facing in a double circle.

ALL FORWARD AND BACK. - - - - - - - - - - - - - 4 measures.

   Couples join inside hands and walk forward toward opposite and return
    moving backwards.

CIRCLE FOUR HANDS AROUND. - - - - - - - - - - 4 „

   Both couples join hands in a circle and move to the left.

RIGHT AND LEFT. - - - - - - - - - - - - - - - - 8 „

   Both couples cross over, the ladies passing between the men. When in op-
    posite place man takes partner's hand in his left and turns her. Return
    to place as before.

LADIES' CHAIN. - - - - - - - - - - - - - - - - 8 measures.

Ladies cross to opposite places giving right hands as they pass each other and left hands to opposite gentlemen, turning once around. They then return to places, giving right hands as they pass and left hands to partners, turning once around.

ALL FORWARD AND BACK. - - - - - - - - - - - - 4 ,,

ALL FORWARD AND PASS THROUGH. - - - - - - - - 4 ,,

Couples join inside hands, walk forward to meet opposite couple, drop hands and pass on to meet a new couple. The ladies pass between the gentlemen.

Repeat the whole dance from the beginning.

Virginia Reel*

American

Victor 18552

Formation - Sets of eight in two lines about four feet apart; partners opposite, all facing center. (№ 1 in one line. № 2 in other line.)

Step   Skip step or walking step.

№ 1 or head couple and 2 of foot couple lead in each figure. №2 of head couple and 1 of foot couple repeat the figure.

Figure 1   Balance corners. Forward to center, bow to partner and backward to position.

"   2   Forward to center, join right hands and turn. Backward to position.

        3   Repeat figure, joining left hands.

"   4   Repeat figure, joining both hands.

"   5   Forward to center, pass back to back, right shoulders first, backward to position.

"   6   Repeat figure, passing with left shoulders first.

        7   Head couple join both hands, arms extended, slide-step (slide, close) to foot and back to head of set.

"   8   Head couple hook right arms (or join right hands) and turn one and one-half times to place. Give left hand to neighbor on opposite side and turn once around. Right arm to partner and turn once around. Continue down the line, turning partner and neighbor alternately to the foot of set. Turn partner one and one-half times around and take position for slide step.

"   9   Slide-step to head of set, to foot of set, and back to head.

"   10   Head couple drop hands and all face forward. Head couple lead off turning toward foot of set on outside of set. Others follow, all clapping. At foot, head couple join hands and continue to position at head of line. Face each other, join both hands and form an arch by raising both arms. Other couples follow, taking their own places in line and forming arch. Last couple pass through arch to head of set. All drop hands and take proper distance. Repeat the dance till all couples are in their original position.

DANCES AND SINGING GAMES
GRADE SEVEN
The Badger Gavotte
American

Music published by Joseph Flanner, 211 Grand Avenue, Milwaukee, Wis.

The walking step should be a smooth gliding movement, the ball of the foot touching the floor first, and the heel last, each starting with the outside foot (lady's right and gentleman's left.)

FIRST PART

Open position, nearest hand joined.

Walk forward four steps; count 1-2-3-4 (1 bar).

Face each other, join both hands, waist high, and slide close, slide close, slide close, point (to the gentlemen's left), counts 5-6-7-8 (1 bar).

Turn and repeat all in the opposite direction, starting with outside foot as follows:

Walk forward four steps: counts 1-2-3-4 (1 bar).

Turn, face each other, join both hands, waist high, and with right foot take, slide close, slide close, slide close, point (to gentleman's right) counts 5-6-7-8 (1 bar); 4 bars in all.

SECOND PART

Waltz position: Execute eight slow two-steps, starting with left foot, and repeat all from the beginning.

The Ball Game

For Boys

Music copyright by Will Von Tilzer

Formation: Three columns facing forward.
Play music through six times.
The description is for one unit of three boys.

	1	2	3
	x	o	⊕
	x	o	⊕
	x	o	⊕
	x	o	⊕

INTRODUCTION

All sing first verse of song as an invitation to the audience to join them at the ball game. At words "one, two, three strikes," the right arm is stretched up with fingers indicating the number of strikes. When "you're out" is sung all motion batter out with a wave of the left hand, thumb pointing over left shoulder.

I.

Boy at right of group (Nº 1) becomes batter.

Measure 1-2 Prepares to bat. Pounds home-plate with bat. Swings bat in preparation.

3 Strikes at ball.

4 Returns to position.

Repeat above during entire music. If a wand or bat is used, provide one for every group of three boys. This is passed on to the middle boy after striking at the ball the last time.

Boy in center of group (Nº 2) becomes pitcher.

Measure 1-2 Prepares to pitch. Winds up. Raises left leg.

3 Pitches ball.

4 Returns to position.
Repeat during the entire music.

Boy at left of group (Nº 3) becomes catcher.

Measure 1-2 Crouches down, knees bent and turned out. Signals to pitcher with fingers in front of mit.

3 Receives ball.

4 Returns ball and returns to crouching position.
Repeat during the entire music.

II.

Boy at right becomes catcher.

Measure 1 Crouch position as in 1. Pound mit with right hand.

Points two fingers of right hand diagonally down towards ground as signal to pitcher.

2 Jerks peak of cap down.

3 Receives ball.

4 Returns ball to pitcher and assumes crouch position.
Repeat during the entire music.

Boy in center becomes batter.

Measure 1   Knocks dirt off of first one shoe and then the other by hitting them with bat.

2   Prepares to bat.

3   Strikes

4   Returns to position.

Boy at left of group becomes pitcher.

Repeat pitcher's movements as described in I.

III

Boy at right of group becomes pitcher.

Repeat pitcher's movements as described in I.

Boy in center becomes catcher.

Measure 1   Adjusts mask by putting entire hand over his face, (fingers spread and pointing up) and pushing with heel of hand resting on chin.

Shakes head vociferously at pitcher.

2   Nods head at pitcher in agreement.

3   Receives ball.

4   Returns ball.

Repeat during the entire music.

Boy at left becomes batter.

Repeat movements of batter as described in I.

IV

All three become shortstops.

Measure 1   Legs apart, knees bent, hand resting on knees. With both hands slap thighs six times in rapid succession.

2   Reach to left with hand and stop grounder.

3-4   Return ball and assume first position.

Repeat during the entire music, stopping the ball during the second measure to the right, using both hands, and thereafter alternating left and right.

V

All three become umpires

Measures

1	Umpire bends forward and brushes off home plate.
2	Adjusts mask as did catcher in III.
3	Squares shoulders to adjust chest protector.
4	Folds arm behind back and leans forward expectantly.
5 - 6	Leans to right to see what is happening on bases.
7 - 8	Leans to left.
9 -10	Steps forward right with a stamp, motioning that player is out.
11	Stretches right hand up signalling strike one on batter.
12	Signals strike two on batter.
13-14	Steps forward left declaring runner safe.
15-16	Motions batter out as in Introduction.
	Repeat.

This dance should portray the real spirit of the ball game.

Courtesy of Miss Hortense Burns

Bean Setting *
English Morris Dance

+ tap sticks
⊓ thump sticks on floor

For Boys

INTRO. Once to yourself.

A   DANCE

* *From* "Hinman Gymnastic and Folk Dancing" Vol. IV, Copyright 1924 by Mary Wood Hinman.
A. S. Barnes & Co. Puhlishers

Formation: Longways, six men in a set. Partners facing.

Step. The easiest form of the Morris step, the $\frac{4}{2}$, is used. It consists of a step, followed by a hop on the same foot extending the free foot forward with leg straight. The same thing is then repeated on the other foot. The steps and hops are of even length and when performed, the step looks like a slow step, hop.

A stick about the diameter of a wand and eighteen inches in length is carried in the right hand by every member of the set.

I

Once to yourself. The introduction is played through once while all stand still facing top of room, odd numbers resting sticks upon partners'. All strike sticks on final beat.

II

A music. Ring. All form circle facing clockwise. Dance half way around the circle. Turn and dancing counter clockwise, return to places. Finish longways as in introduction.

III

B music. Dib and Strike. To "dib" is to thrust the end of the stick vertically against the ground, and lift it up again. All dib with sticks as marked in the music on the first and middle beats of the first measure. Partners then strike sticks, passing the strike around as marked in the second measure. No 1 hits No 3's stick who holds it out for him, No 3 hits No 5's; No 5 hits No 6's; No 6 hits No 4's; No 4 hits No 2's.

All hit opposites.

Repeat all.

```
1   2
3   4
5   6
```

IV

A music. Cross Over. This is danced by each pair of partners simultaneously. Partners change places, each passing to the left. Turn toward one another and continue back to own places, still passing to the left.

V

B music. Dib and Strike.

VI

A music. Back to Back. Partners move forward passing to the left, pass one another back to back and return to places.

VII

B music. Dib and Strike.

VIII

A music. Hey. See English Folk Dance Terms. Grade IV.

IX

B music. Dib and Strike. Finish with crossed sticks, facing up.

Bow Wow

American

This dance comes from the eastern slope of the Adirondack Mountains not far from Lake George, New York. All calls are in quotation marks.

Formation: Four couples facing in quadrille formation.

```
        1
        OX

2 X        O 4
  O        X

      XO
      3
```

I

a. "Hands eight" All join hands and circle left.

b. "Hands four" Couples one and two join hands and circle left.

c. "Ladies join hands" The first and second girls join hands.

"Gents join hands" The first and second boys join both hands across the joined hands of the girls.

"Ladies bow-wow" First and second girls slip heads under arms of boys as the boys swing arms over.

"Gents bow-wow" First and second boys slip their heads under girls' arms.

"And around you go" In this basket formation the four slide to the left fast and furiously.

d. Repeat b and c with couples three and four.

e. "Allemande left" Swing neighbor with buzz steps.

f. "Grand right and left."

g. "Promenade" All slide sideways around set, each couple in social dancing position.

II

Repeat all of I except a, with couple two starting the figures.

III

Repeat all of I except a, with couple three starting the figures.

IV

Repeat all of I except a, with couple four starting the figures.

Clogs

The following clogs may be found in Frost "The Clog Dance Book."

Irish Jig

Liza Jane

Reuben Taps

English Dances

The following dances may be obtained at any music store or from H. W. Gray & Co., N.Y.

Rufty Tufty

The Old Mole

Donegal Country Dance

pronounced Dun-e-gaul'

Irish

The White Cockade

Donegal is a county in the North of Ireland.

Danced to Reel Time.

Formation: Partner dance, single circle; ladies on right of their partners.

I. Beat Round

Take hands all round in ring, dance to left (2 bars), set (2 bars), dance back to right (2 bars), set (2 bars).

II. Turn Ladies.

Gentlemen take both hands of ladies on left, turn them (4 bars), release hands, return to own partners, take both hands, turn in place (4 bars).

III. Link Arms.

Gentlemen link right arms with ladies on left, turn (2 bars), return to own partners with left arms, turn (2 bars), return to ladies on left with right arms, turn (2 bars), back again to own partners with left arms, turn in place (2 bars).

IV. Lead Round.

Gentlemen place right hand on partners' left shoulder taking her left hand in his left, lead round in circle thus (16 bars); commence dance again in whatever position you finish.

From "A Handbook of Irish Dances" *by* O'Keefe and O'Brien.

The Hatter
Hattemageren
Danish

Victor 18000

Music: ‖: 1-8 :‖: 9-16 :‖: 17-24 :‖

Original Position: Four couples in quadrille formation.

Steps: Buzz steps in swings, otherwise skip step.

First Figure: (a) Big circle clockwise (1-8, 1-8)

(b) Dancers release hands, partners face each other and stamp three times, (left, right, left,) then clap hands three times (9-12). Again three stamps and three claps (13-16). Ladies and gentlemen turn to strange ladies and gentlemen, stamp and clap three times, again three stamps and three claps (9-16).

(c) Chain once around (17-24, 17-24); (grand right and left).

Second Figure: (a) Dance in place with partner, buzz steps.

Third, Fifth, and Seventh Figures: (a) Ladies form circle, clasping hands behind waists of others, making a "basket" and dance round sunwise, buzz steps.

Fourth, Sixth, and Eighth Figures: (a) Gentlemen the same.

Ninth Figure: (a) Big circle clockwise. (b) and (c) are alike in all figures.

Finish by dancing in place with own lady, buzz steps.

Hungarian Czardas

Pronounced Char dash

Hungarian Folk Song
Ritka Buza

The description given below was obtained from the Hungarian colony in Detroit. The Czardas, the national dance of Hungary, is always a social, couple dance. According to the members of the Hungarian Colony, it is never done as a solo dance. In fact, solo dancing is found only in cafes, cabarets, or on the stage. There are a great many Czardas tunes, just as in this country there are many fox-trots. The one given above is the old Hungarian folk-song, Ritka Buza. "Ritka" is a girl's name meaning "rare" and "Buza" means "wheat". The song is a play on the word "Ritka." According to it, good wheat is very rare, so also it is very rare to find a nice little girl.

Formation. Couples scattered about the room. Boy's hands on girl's waist. Girl's hands on boy's shoulders.

The following directions are for the boy.

1 Measure. Short step to the right, close left, step right in place, touch left. Step left, close right, step left, touch right.

This is repeated indefinitely moving about the room, progressing either forward or sideward.

8 Measures. At the dancers' will, the following turn may be taken. Keeping the same position of arms, they turn so that right shoulders are together. Leaning away from one another, they swing vigorously clockwise with ordinary walking steps.

This turn may be reversed, so that the dancers move counter-clockwise if the dancers desire.

Irish Long Dance

Top of Cork Road

Victor 17840

Formation: Sets of 2 couples, partners facing.

Measures 1 Touch R toe in front of L (hop L) swing R foot around in back of L (hop) put weight on R foot.

,, 2 Four tiny steps in place beginning L, feet crossed, with R in back of L. Steps executed on toes.

,, 3 - 4 Repeat Measures 1 and 2 to the left.

,, 5 - 8 Whole set joins R hands in pin wheel. Four polkas, around to left.

,, 1 - 8 (repeated) Repeat Measures 1-8 beginning left foot.

,, 9-10 Couple Nº 1 joins hands and takes 4 slides down between Couple Nº 2.

,, 11 - 12 Four slides back to place.

,, 13-14 Couple Nº 1 four slides down set while Couple Nº 2 slides up on outside.

,, 15-16 Repeat Measures 13-14 with Couple Nº 2 passing inside while Couple Nº 1 return to places on outside.

,, 1 - 8 Girl places hands on partner's shoulders, boy on girl's waist.

    8 Polkas executed in small circle, couples moving counter-clockwise turning one and one-half time so that at the end of the 8 polkas the couples have changed places.

    Repeat entire dance and finish with Couple Nº 1 in original place.

The Lancers
American

FIGURE I

Address partners, then corners.

First four forward and back, and turn the opposite .... 8 bars

    Give both hands in turning the opposite.

First couple promenade between the opposite, and return on the outside. .... 8 ,,

All balance corners, turn partners .... 8 ,,

Side couples forward and back, and turn the opposite .... 8 ,,

The next couple promenade between the opposite, return on the outside. .... 8 ,,

All balance corners, turn partners .... 8 ,,

Repeat all. Play four times.

FIGURE 2

Wait first eight measures.

First four forward and back, ladies cross over .... 8 bars

    Ladies cross over and stand beside the opposite gentlemen.

Chasse 4   ,,

    Ladies join nearest hands with new partner, and all slide four steps to the right side, then four steps to the left side.

Cross back to partner 4   ,,

All join hands, forward, turn partners 8   ,,

Side four forward and back, ladies cross over.. 8   ,,

Chasse 4   ,,

Cross back to partner 4   ,,

All join hands, forward, turn partners.. 8   ,,

Repeat all, the gentlemen crossing over. Play four times

FIGURE 3

Wait first eight measures.

First four forward and back .... 4 bars

Forward again and address 4   ,,

Ladies chain 8   ,,

Side four forward and back 4   ,,

Forward again and address 4   ,,

Ladies chain 8   ,,

All join hands, forward and back 4   ,,

Forward again and address 4   ,,

Four ladies grand chain... 8   ,,

FIGURE 4

Wait first eight measures

First four lead to the right, address .... 4 bars

Lead to the left, address 4   ,,

Return to place, address partner 4   ,,

First four right and left.. 8   ,,

Side four lead to the right, address 4   ,,

Lead to the left, address.. 4   ,,

Return to place, address partner.. 4   ,,

Side four right and left 8   ,,

Repeat all, leading to left hand couples. Play four times.

* For description of this movement see p. 168

FIGURE 5

Before the orchestra begins, call ADDRESS PARTNERS. The chord is then given by the orchestra and all address each other. Then call the first change, after which the orchestra begins.

Grand right and left	16 bars
The first couple face out	8 "
Chasse. (Slide four steps away from set, and return.)	8 "
All march (Counter-clockwise around set with partner.)	8 "
All forward, turn partners	8 "
Grand right and left	16 "
Next couple face out	8 "
Chasse	8 "
All march	8 "
All forward, turn partners	8 "
The grand square, first four forward, sides separate	8 "
Sides forward, first four separate	8 "
The next couple face out	8 "
Chasse	8 "
March	8 "
All forward, turn partners	8 "
The grand square, sides forward, first four separate	8 "
First four forward, sides separate	8 "
The last couple, face out	8 "

Always in this change, the couple cross hands and promenade eight steps inside the set before facing out.

Chasse	8 "
March	8 "
All forward, turn partners	8 "
All join hands forward and back	4 "
Forward again and address	4 "
All promenade to seats	8 "

Lindy Lee*

From Hinman "Gymnastic and Folk Dancing" Vol. V. copyright by Mary Wood Hinman, A.S. Barnes & Co.
publishers.

I

Fall down stairs." 7 counts to left and back 7 counts.   4 measures.

Face left, weight on right foot, left leg raised backward, body bent forward, arms forward.

Two steps backward (left, right)

Half turn right and 2 steps forward (left, right)

Half turn left and 2 steps backward (left, right)

Half turn right and 1 step forward left, hold.

Repeat beginning right foot.

(Relax, left knee high and tumble.)

(Take steps in a straight line. The turn is always toward the front.)

II

5 left, brush right heel to the left, hop left and place right heel to the left side. 2 measures.

(Clap Lands with the hop, arms sideward (hands vertical) with the heel placing, turn left as heel is placed, right hand over right foot.)

Repeat right. 2 measures.

III

Deep knee bend, arms crossed.

Rise, touch left sideward, arms sideward.

With hop, half turn right touch left sideward. Repeat twice $\frac{1}{4}$ turn each time.

Repeat deep knee and turn to the left. 4 measures in all.

IV

"Wiggle-sticks" 2 slow, 4 fast.

(Place toes together, heels out. With one movement turn left toe out, place right foot back of left toe to heel of left.) 1 measure. Repeat.

Repeat four times, double time. 2 measures.

V

(a) Step swing forward left, right, left, right. Repeat backward.

(b) Step backward left, together; forward left, together. Leap forward left, right. Repeat.

VI

"Rubber Legs"

(a) Weight on left foot, crossed in front; change weight to right, change weight to left and cut right to side; cut left to side.

(4 counts.) 1 measure.

Repeat

(b) Toe kick left, right, left, right.

VII

"Break your leg."

Turn left, deep knee left, right leg straight (lunge position with weight forward.) Repeat to right.

Repeat left, right, left, quick time - hold 4th count. 2 measures in all.

VIII

Fall down stairs to left, starting back with right foot. 2 measures.

Russian Scherr (Knife)

Russian Folk Tune

Sets of four couples, quadrille formation.

I

In a circle, all hands joined shoulder high; move in circle to left with seven slow, strong (stamp) steps. A music.

Repeat to right. Couples drop back to own places in the square.

II

Cross over or cut. B music (repeated)

1. Couples 1 and 3 exchange places, gentlemen leading ladies across with four walking steps. Drop hands, ladies "cut" through opposite couple. Both couples face each other again, taking four steps backward to other couple's place.
Couples 2 and 4 stamp and clap in place.

2. Couples 2 and 4 exchange places in same way, while couples 1 and 3 stamp and clap in place.

III

Visits. (A and B music)

1. While the others stamp and clap in place, the lady of couple № 1 and gentleman of № 2 move toward each other with step right, stamp left, step left, stamp right. Gentleman places hands on lady's hips; lady places hands on his shoulders. They swing around to left with four "buzzing" steps. Lady № 1 and gentleman № 2 go back to own partners.

2. All repeat above movement with own partners.   A music.

1. Lady N⁰ 1 repeats step with gentleman N⁰ 3.

2. Repeat 2. B music.

1. Lady N⁰ 1 repeats step with gentleman N⁰ 4.

2. Repeat 2. B music (repeated).

2. Repeat whole dance until ladies N⁰ 2, 3, 4, have each had a turn to visit.

Then, if desired, gentlemen may take turns.

University High Clog *

* *From* Hinman "Gymnastic and Folk Dancing" vol. V. copyright by Mary Wood Hinman, A. S. Barnes & Co.,
publishers

Measures

1. 7 - 7 - 3 - 7 Stamp, stamp. . . . . .1 - 4

2. 7 - 7 - 3 - 7 Stamp, stamp. . . . . .Repeated 1 - 4

3. 7 - 7 - 3 - 3 - 7 . . . . .5 - 8

4. 7 - 7 - 3 - 7 Stamp, stamp. 9-12

5. "Wiggle-sticks"

Turn toes in, touching each other.

Turn toes out, placing left toe at right heel.

Turn toes in,

Turn toes out, placing right toe at left heel.   Measures

This is done slowly for 2 measures, then double quick for 2 measures.   13-16

6. "Down the field" to the left (i.e., step on left foot and push with right foot, turn-

ing toe in on push) 4 times. Repeat right 17-20

7. "Wiggle-sticks" 13-16

8. "Down the field" to the left for 2 measures 17-18

5 little jumps.

   1. With feet together pointing to the left.

   2. With feet together pointing to the right.

   3. With feet together pointing to the left.

   4. With feet together pointing ahead.

   5. Jump high in the air. 21-22

GRADE EIGHT

Birdie in the Center

American

Oh! Susanna
Stephen C. Foster

Although this dance is found on both the Canadian and American sides of the Detroit River and Lake St. Clair it has been included as an American dance because it has so many characteristics of other American dances. The name has been taken from one of the calls since it is given no name by those who dance it.

Formation: Quadrille

I

a. "Honor your partners right and left." Bow first to your partner, then to your neighbor.

b. "Join hands all." Circle left half-way around.

"Promenade back." Men give girls their right arms. Return to place.

c. "Head couple down the center and cut off six." Head couple joins inside hands, passes down the center of the set, passes through the foot couple, separtes, passes behind side couples and returns to place.   (See diagram 1.)

"Swing your partner when you meet." Head couple swings with buzz steps.

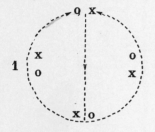 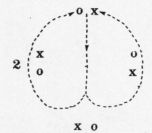 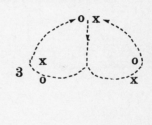

d. "Head couple down the center and cut off four."

Head couple with hands joined passes down center, separates, man going to left   between foot couple and side couple.   Girl does the same to the right   Pass behind side couples as in c, and return to place. (See diagram 2.)

"Swing your partner when you meet." As in c.

e. "Head couple down the center and cut off two."

Head couple passes down the center, separates, man passes through couple N⁰ 4, girl through couple N⁰ 2. (Diagram 3)

"Whole set swings."

f. "Allemande left."

Men swing women on their left once around. Grand right and left until partners meet. (Half way around circle.)

"Promenade back to place." (See b.)

All figures of I may be repeated with each couple if desired.

II

a. "Birdie in the center, three hands around."

   (Birdie is the head woman.) Head couple leads to couple N⁰ 2. Head man joins hands with couple N⁰ 2. Head woman in center of circle. Circle progresses around to left.

b. "Birdie flies out and hockie flies in."

   ("Hockie" is the head man.) Repeat a. with man in center.

c. "Hockie flies out and gives Birdie a swing." Head couple swings.

d. Head couple repeats same figure with foot couple.

e. Head couple repeats same figure with couple N⁰ 4.

f. "Allemande left."

III

a. "All join hands."

   All join hands, move towards center of circle, back to places. Men swing girls on their left. Swing partners.

b. "Gentlemen! Take that lady by the wrist and lead around with a grape vine twist, around the gent with a grape twine dance, four hands round with a jolly prance."

   Head man takes partner by the wrist and leads her to second couple, passes through second couple, around girl, then around the man of the second couple. (See Diagram) The two couples join hands and circle.

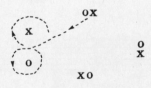

c. Head couple with couple two following, hands joined in a line, repeats figure with couple three.

   All circle six hands around (three couples)

d. Couples one, two, and three, repeat entire figure with couple four. Circle eight hands around until back in original places.

e. "Allemande left."

f. Repeat III a.

   All figures in III may be repeated with each couple acting as head couple. If this is done figure f. is not danced until all couples have completed the "grape vine."

The Butcher's Dance*

Resnicka

Czecho Slovakian

This dance represents a butcher buying an ox from a farmer. In A, measures 9-12 they are bickering about the price.

Formation: Partners in a double circle, moving counter-clockwise, girl on the right. The music consists of two parts, A of sixteen measures and B of eight measures, which is repeated. In fitting the steps to the music, each measure should be counted, "one, two"

A

Measures 1 - 8 Social dancing position, boy's right arm around girl's waist, outside hands clasped, elbows straight. Beginning with the outside foot and turning continuously right, all take eight Czeck polka steps (step, close, step.)

9   Partners release each other, the girl steps around in front of her part- ner, making a single circle. Boy rests girls right hand, palm upward, in his left.

10   With a large movement he slaps it with his right.

11 - 12 Repeat measures 9 -10, the girl slapping the boy's hand.

13 - 16 Repeat measures 9 -12.

1 B

During 1 B, partners take two running steps to each measure, the girl moving backward beginning left and the boy forward beginning right.

Measure 1   Clap hands together (one), clap partner's hand (two)

2   Clap hands together (one), clap partner's right (two)

3   Clap hands (one), clap partner's left (two)

4   Clap hands (one) clap partner's hand (two)

5 - 8 Repeat measures 13 -16

2 B

Measure 1 - 8 Repeat 1 B, girl moving forward, and boy backward.

Captain Jinks Square Dance
American

This dance comes from the eastern slope of the Adirondack Mountains not far from Lake George, New York. While the calls are perhaps crude in places, they have been included to retain the old spirit of the dance. They are found in quotation marks and the teacher may use them or not at her discretion.

The music for this dance will be found in Grade IV. "Captain Jinks."

Formation: Four couples in quadrille formation.

I

a. "Hands eight." All join hands and circle left.

b. "First lady turns with Mr. Jinks." With buzz steps the first woman turns with the second man.

"First lady turns the man with the drinks." First woman turns with the third man as before.

"First lady turns the man who doesn't drink." First woman turns with the fourth man as before.

"First lady turns the bum of the hall." First woman turns with her partner.

c. "Allemande left." Swing neighbors once.

d. "Grand right and left." Give right hands to partners first.

e. "All promenade." In social dancing position slide sidewise around set and return to places.

f. Repeat all from I B with second, third, and fourth women turning the men of the set as the first woman did.

II

a. "First man turns with Mrs. Jinks." First man turns second woman with buzz steps.

"First man turns the lady with rats in her hair." First man turns third woman as before.

"First man turns the lady who doesn't paint." First man turns fourth woman.

"First man turns the belle of the ball." First man turns his partner.

b. "Allemande left."

c. "Grand right and left."

d. "All promenade."

e. Repeat all of II with second, third, and fourth men turning the woman as did the first man.

"Run away home" or "Promenade to you know where." Take your partner to a seat.

Irish Waltz Clog
On Deck

The above clogs are recommended for this grade. The music and description are in Frost "The Clog Dance Book."

The Crested Hen

Den Toppede Hone

Danish

Formation: One gentleman and two ladies.

Skip step.

a. Dancers circle sunwise (1-8) and contra-sunwise (1-8). Stamp on beginning and at the turning.

b. Ladies release hands, place free hand on hip. Right lady dances through arch formed by two others; she is followed by gentleman, who dances under his own lifted arm, still holding ladies' hands. Now left lady dances through arch formed by the two others, followed by gentleman (9-16) Repeat (9-16)

Repeat and continue as long as desired.

Dance of the Hottentots

For Boys

Music and description in Frost, "The Clog Dance Book."

Fryksdals Polska
Swedish

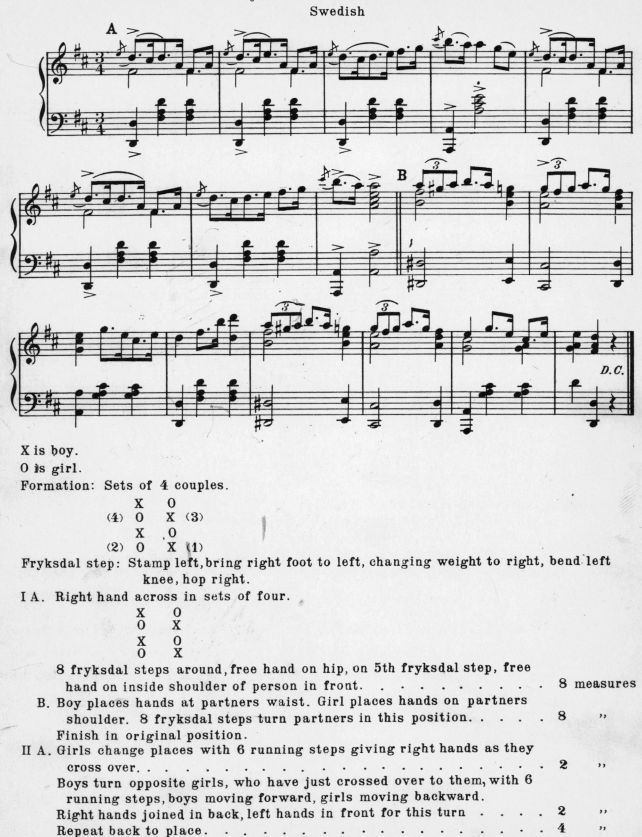

X is boy.

O is girl.

Formation: Sets of 4 couples.

```
        X   O
 (4)  O       X  (3)
        X   O
 (2)  O       X  (1)
```

Fryksdal step: Stamp left, bring right foot to left, changing weight to right, bend left
knee, hop right.

I A. Right hand across in sets of four.

```
        X   O
      O       X
      X       O
        O   X
```

8 fryksdal steps around, free hand on hip, on 5th fryksdal step, free
hand on inside shoulder of person in front. . . . .   8 measures

B. Boy places hands at partners waist. Girl places hands on partners
shoulder. 8 fryksdal steps turn partners in this position. . . . .   8 ”
Finish in original position.

II A. Girls change places with 6 running steps giving right hands as they
cross over. . . . .   2 ”

Boys turn opposite girls, who have just crossed over to them, with 6
running steps, boys moving forward, girls moving backward.

Right hands joined in back, left hands in front for this turn . . . .   2 ”

Repeat back to place. . . . .   4 ”

Repeat I B. Finish in original formation.

III A   X   O   (4)   (3)
        (4) O   X   (3)   O X O X
                 X   O   X O X O
        (2) O   X   (1)   (2)   (1)

Join hands in lines of four

6 running steps forward . . . . 2 meas.

6 running steps backward . . . . 2 ,,

6 running steps forward . . . . 2 ,,

Drop hands in middle of lines

Join hands at ends, swinging back in new lines with 6 running steps. . . 2 ,,

B. Repeat I B. Move in toward center on this turn ready for next formation.

IV A. Pinwheels of eight, boys giving right hands across, girls take boys' left arms.

8 fryksdal steps around . . . . 8 ,,

Boys swing girls in so that girls give left hands across

Boys take girls' right arms . . . . 8 ,,

Girls swing boys in . . . . 4 ,,

Boys swing girls in . . . . 4 ,,

B Repeat I B.

Finish facing forward in sets of four, partners inside hands joined.

        (4) ↑ O = X O X (3)
        (2) | O = X O - X (1)

V A. Couples 2 and 4 make arches first while boy of couple 1 starts line running
    underneath them   Girl in couple 1 takes hand of boy in couple 3 so that all
    face in same direction. As girl of couple 3 passes under arch 2, she takes
    free hand of boy in couple 2. Girl in couple 2 takes free hand of boy in
    couple 4 completing the chain. When couples 1 and 3 have reached their
    own places they form arches for couples 2 and 4 who pass thru and back
    to their own places. . . . . 16 meas.

A running step is used throughout the figure whether moving or in place.

B. Repeat all, girl in couple 2 starting the chain and couples 1 and 3 making
   the arches first. 16 ,,

VI A.   (4) O X   O X (3)
             (2) O X   O X (1)

Couples who formed arches together give right hands across in pinwheel.
Repeat I A.

B Repeat I B. Hold final position for good finish.
  Fryksdal step starts on left foot throughout the dance. Step left (1), step
  right foot to left changing weight to right (2), bend left knee hopping on
  right foot as in mazurka (3).

Flamborough Sword*

English

Victor 17847- Columbia A 7529

Rapidly. *Play with marked even rhythm*

***From** Hinman "Gymnastic and Folk Dancing" vol. V. copyright by Mary Wood Hinman. A.S. Barnes & Co. publishers.

The swords are made of ash or larch, 37 inches long, and $1\frac{1}{2}$ inches wide, shaped into a handle at one end and tapering at the other.

N⁰ 1 is Sword Master or leader. Enter in single file formation, thus: Sword Master N⁰ 1 followed by 8, 7, 6, 5, 4, 3, 2. A simple vigorous skip is used throughout the dance and is maintained even when marking time in stationary position.

Entrance

Skip into a circle moving clock-wise. Hold sword in left hand with the blade of the sword resting against left shoulder, right hand at side.

I

Sixteen skips in the circle going clock-wise, men about three paces apart. Extend sword over left shoulder and with right hand grasp the point of the sword held by the man in front. This joins the circle, and is completed in sixteen skips.

II

Circle and Lock

Swing own sword overhead and pull hands apart. Push the hilt of sword held in left hand under the sword point of the dancer who stands at the left. Each boy has pulled his left hand to the left, his right hand to the right, thus crossing the two swords he is holding. By pushing the hilt of the left sword under the point of the sword at the left and at the same time allowing the man on the right to put his hilt under the right point, a star is formed. This star is called a "lock" and is made of the locked swords of the eight dancers.

III

Lifted Lock

Leader lifts the lock shoulder high and all continue with sixteen steps around the circle.

IV

Clash

On the first beat of the measure, lower the lock into the center of the circle hip high and each member of the group grasps his own hilt with left hand. Hold the lock in this position while continuing to skip sixteen counts clock-wise. When the sword master shouts "Draw," every man pulls his own sword from the lock, raises it high overhead. All clash swords for sixteen counts with swords held above the heads, like a tent. The skipping continues in circle formation which has necessarily grown smaller, as the men have closed in to strike each others swords.

V

Threedling

Lower swords and gradually enlarge the circle as each man catches the point of his right hand neighbor's sword with his right hand. The group is in "hilt and point position" and a large circle is formed with very vigorous skipping steps as the swords are extended hip-high between the dancers.   Sixteen counts.

(a)   The sword master turns and faces No. 8 who stands immediately behind him. They lower No. 8's sword which is held in the sword master's right hand and No. 8's left hand. No. 8 raises his right hand in which is grasped the point of No. 7's sword, turns to his left and jumps over the lowered sword, and continues dancing to his left followed by the group who in succession leap over the lowered sword still held by No. 8 and the sword master. Swords are again lifted to outside shoulder, circle is now facing counter-clockwise and in this direction they skip sixteen counts.

(b)   No. 2 now faces sword master and they raise the sword between them. Sword master raises his left hand and passes under his own sword. The sword is kept raised while all of the group pass under. The circle is now skipping clockwise. (After the master has passed under his raised sword, he must move to his right.)

(c)   Sword master faces No. 8 and repeats step with the sword raised instead of lowered. Sixteen counts.

(d)   Repeat step b sixteen counts.

VI

Double Threedling

Circle breaks. All retain own swords, held as in entrance step, and fall into two lines. No. 5 facing No. 6; No. 4 facing No. 7; No. 3 facing No. 8; and at the head of the line No. 2 facing the sword master. Continue skipping step on spot.

(a)   No. 2 and the sword master simultaneously turn to their own left, and cast down the set with eight skipping steps. The sword master skips down the outside and No. 2 skips down between the two lines of men. The sword master returns to his place up the center and No. 2 returns up the outside of his own line. No. 2 and the sword master present their swords across to one another, each grasping the point of the other sword with the right hand, thus making a double arch of swords. Keeping the wrists and swords parallel they roll under these swords by turning twice with the skip step under this lifted arch of swords. At the close of the step, they fall into position at bottom of set, and dropping partner's sword, replace own on left shoulder. Sixteen counts. This is repeated by each couple in turn until No. 2 and the sword master are against at the head.

(b)   All swords extended across and grasped by partner, thus forming double arch of swords held high over head. First couple turns under lifted swords to position at foot of set, eight counts, followed by each successive couple.

VII

Weaving or Shuttle Step

Still grasping the point of the opposite man's sword all lower swords to hip level. The sword master and No. 2 begin the new step by the sword master pushing his partner backward four counts. At the same time No. 8 pulls his partner forward four counts. On the next four counts, they exchange places. Couples Nos. 4 and 7, move in the same direction as couples Nos. 3 and 8. Couples Nos. 5 and 6 and couples Nos. 4 and 7 exchange places at the same time and in the same manner as the two leading couples. Couples Nos. 3 and 8 are now leading couples. They turn outward under their own swords on spot in eight counts, while couples Nos. 4 and 7 repeat at the opposite end by turning outward on spot eight times. Simultaneously couples Nos. 5 and 6 and No. 2 and sword master change places in the center. This continues until all the couples have been up and down the line once. (In going down the line, left file of dancers push partners forward. In going up the file, left file push partners backward.) On reaching either end, every couple turns outward on spot under own swords twice, for eight counts.

VIII

Hey

The dancers release partner's swords but retain own swords in left hand on left shoulder. Skip into a long line, in no regular order facing the sword master. The sword master now dances down the entire line by passing alternately to the right and to the left of each man in the group. (A grand right and left, only no hands are used.) All dancers should go down and up the line at least once. On reaching original place, the sword master steps out from the group and as each man comes to the head of the line, he calls out his number and he dances into a straight line behind him, until the last man skips into the line.

IX

Repeat Entrance Step

X

Repeat Circle Step, and Lock Step.

After forming lock, sword master holds the woven swords on high and shouts "break;" the circle of men break between five and four, falling back into a straight line with the sword master near center, holding the lock on high. The dancers come forward, turn to their right and follow off behind No. 4.

From Hinman "Gymnastic & Folk Dances" vol. V. copyright by Mary Wood Hinman, A. S. Barnes & Co., publishers.

The Girl I Left Behind Me
American

This dance comes from the eastern slope of the Adirondack Mountains, not far from Lake George, New York. All calls are in quotation marks. The music for this is Irish. It is not known whether this dance originally came from Ireland, or whether the Americans, having little music of their own, used this Irish tune for their dance.

Formation: Four couples facing in quadrille formation.

I

a. "Hands eight" All join hands and circle left.

b. "Hands four" Couples one and two join hands and circle left.

c. "Then pass right through, balance to, and swing the girl behind you." Couples one and two facing one another, move forward and pass through, the girls passing through the center.

The first man turns and swings the second girl with buzz steps while the second man swings the first girl. Finish with second girl beside first man and first girl beside second man.

d. "Then go right back on the same old track and swing the girl behind you." First man takes second girl, second man takes first girl, pass through as before, turn and swing original partner.

e. First couple repeats b, c and d, with third and fourth couples.

f. "Allemande left"   Swing neighbor.

g. "Grand right and left."

h. "Promenade" All slide sideways around set each couple in social dancing position.

II

Repeat all of I. except a, with couple two starting the figures.

III

Repeat all of I. except a, with couple three starting the figures.

IV

Repeat all of I. except a, with couple four starting the figures.

Highland Fling*
Scotch

Victor 17001

*From Hinman "Gymnastic and Folk Dancing" vol. V. copyright by Mary Wood Hinman. A.S. Barnes & Co. publishers.

I. a. Count 1 Spring on toes

           ”   2   Hop on left, lift right foot behind left knee.

           ”   3   Hop again on left bringing right foot in front of left knee.

           ”   4   Same as 2.

           ”   5-6-7-8   Repeat all to right.

           ”   9-10-11-12   Same as 1-4.

           ”   13   Same as 1.

           ”   14   Hop on right turning $\frac{1}{3}$ around to right, bringing left foot up in front.

           ”   15   Hop on right turning $\frac{1}{3}$ around to right, to face toward the back, bringing left foot up behind.

           ”   16   Hop on right turning $\frac{1}{3}$ around to right, to face forward, bringing left foot up in front.

    b. Repeat all opposite 1-16.

II. Touch and Lift Step.

    a. 1 and 2 same as I. (a) above.

      3 Hop on left, right foot pointed in front.

      4 Hop on left, right foot lifted in front of left knee.

      5-8 Repeat opposite.

      9-12 Same as 1-4.

      13-16 Same as 13-16 in I. (a.)

    b. Repeat all opposite 1-16.

III. Heel and Toe.

    a. 1 and 2 as in I. (a)

      3 Hop on left, right heel touches in front.

      4 Hop on left again, right toe pointed in front.

      5-8 Repeat opposite.

      9-12 Same as 1-4

      13-16 Same as 13-16 in I. (a)

    b. Repeat all opposite 1-16.

IV. Combination.

    a. 1-4 Same as in I. (a)

      5-8 Same as 1-4 in II. (a)

      9-12 Same as 5-8 in I. (a)

      13-16 Same as in 5-8 in II. (a)

b. 1 - 4   Same as **13-16** in I. (b)

    5 - 8   Same as **1-4** in II. (a)

    9-12   Same as **13-16** in I. (a)

    13-16   Same as **5-8** in II. (a)

V   Traveling

  a 1   Hop on left, right toe pointed in front.

    2   Hop on left, lift right foot in front on left knee.

    3   Step backward right.

    4   Step backward left.

    5-8 Repeat **1-4** starting with opposite foot.

    9-12 Repeat **1-4**.

    13-16 Four steps backward.

  b. Repeat all opposite **1-16**.

VI. Spring and turn.

  a. 1   Spring on both toes.

    2   Hop on left, bringing right foot up behind left knee.

    3   Same as **1**.

    4   Hop on right bringing left foot up behind right knee.

    5-8   Same as **1-4** in I. (a)

    9-12   Repeat **1-4** above opposite.

    13-16   Same as **13-16** in I. (a)

  b. Repeat all opposite **1-16**.

VII. Turn

  a. 1 - 4   Same as **13-16** in I. (a)

    5 - 8   Repeat.

    9-12   Repeat.

    13-16   4 Steps backward.

  b. Repeat all opposite **1-16**.

From Hinman "Gymnastic & Folk Dancing" copyright by Mary Wood Hinman, A.S. Barnes & Co., publishers.

The Irish Lilt

From Crampton "The Folk Dance Book" copyright 1909 by A. S. Barnes & Co., publishers.

Steps

1 Forward Rock.	4. Leg Twist and Kick.
2. Kick.	5. Side Step.
3. Toe and Heel.	6. Kick and Change.

Break - a connecting step

Before teaching this dance the preliminary step, Sideward Rock, may be used to advantage to establish the rhythm.

Sideward Rock: From position with heels together and hands at sides, on count one, hop and raise right leg sideways. On count two, hop and bring right leg under body and raise left leg sideways. One measure.

Repeat rapidly to music.

I

Forward Rock: Similar to "Sideward Rock" except that plane of movement is changed from sideward to forward and back. On count one, hop with weight on left foot, raising right foot backward. On count two, hop on right foot and raise left foot forward, one measure. Repeat up to twelve counts (six measures) always raising left foot forward and right foot backward.

After the twelfth count, by means of the "Break" (one measure) bring the right foot forward and repeat the step with "Break."

Break: On count one, spring and spread feet. On count two, spring and bring feet together again. On count three, hop and raise left leg backward. On count four, hop and kick left leg forward. Two measures.

Practice this movement thoroughly. After having learned it, the "Break" is not used as a separate step but is used to connect the various steps, and to connect the first and second halves of each step. For example, when the twelfth count in the first half of 'Forward Rock' is reached, the left foot is forward in the air; the feet should then be spread (count one of the 'Break'), brought together again (count two), the right leg raised in back (count three) then brought forward (count four), ready to be placed on the ground for the first count of the second half of the 'Forward Rock' which is done with the right foot forward. The same process is gone through with at the end of the step in order to bring the left leg in position to start the next step.

II

Kick: Two counts to each foot. On count one, spring and raise left leg backward. On count two, spring and kick left leg forward outward. On count three, spring to left and raise right leg backward. On count four, spring and kick right leg forward outward. Continue to twelfth count (six measures) then do 'Break' for four counts (two measures) then repeat step with 'Break.'

III

Toe and Heel: Four counts to each side. Twelve counts- six measures. On count one spring and face to right, stretching left leg backward but to left of starting position and placing left toe on floor. On count two, spring and about face to left, rotating left leg and placing left heel where toe was. On count three, spring and face to front, placing left toe on floor near right foot. On count four, spring and kick left leg forward outward. On count five, spring and land on left leg, facing to left with right leg extended and toe on floor. On count six, seven and eight, proceed as with left leg. On counts nine to twelve, repeat with left leg. Then 'Break' and start with right leg for twelve more counts (six mesures) and 'Break.'

IV

Leg Twist and Kick: Similar to the 'Toe and Heel' except that the toe and heel of extended leg are not placed on the floor. The pointing out of this similarity will aid in teaching the step. Four counts to each side. Twelve counts- six measures. On count one, spring and face to right, raising left leg backwards. On count two, spring and about face to left, rotating left leg, but keeping it pointed in same direction, with knee slightly bent. On count three, spring and place left toe near right foot. On count four, spring and kick left leg outward. On count five, spring to left foot and face to left, raising right leg backward. On counts six, seven and eight, same as with left leg. On counts nine to twelve, with right leg. Then 'Break' four counts- two measures. Repeat, starting with left leg.

V

Side Step: Eight steps to two counts- one measure, instead of four as in the other 'Steps'. On count one, place left leg across in front of right leg and left foot on floor to right of right foot. On count two, place right foot to right of left foot, but in back. On count three, again move left foot past right to right. On count four, again move right foot past left to right. On count five again move left foot past right to right. On count six, again move right foot past left to right. On count seven, again move left foot past right to right. On count eight hop on left foot and slightly backward, swinging the right leg forward. On count nine place right foot to left of left foot in front. On count ten, move left foot to left. On counts eleven to fifteen, proceed as in first seven counts, but toward the left, starting the right foot in front. On count sixteen, hop on right foot and swing left leg forward. On counts seventeen to twenty-four as in first eight counts. Then 'Break' and bring right leg forward and proceed for twenty-four counts- twelve measures.

The idea in this step is to take short steps sideways very rapidly, changing direction every eighth count with a hop.

VI

Kick and Change: On count one, spring and place left toe back of right heel. On count two, spring and kick left leg diagonally forward. On count three, spring and place weight on left foot and raise right leg backward. On count four, hop with left leg, and still hold right leg up in back. On count five, hop with left leg, and place right toe back of left heel. On count six, spring and kick right leg diagonally forward. On count seven, spring to right and raise left leg backward. On count eight, hop with right foot, holding right leg up in back. On counts nine to twelve, as in first four counts. Then 'Break' and repeat, starting with right toe. Each step should start to the left and continue for twelve beats. Then the 'Break' should come in for four beats bringing the right leg forward; the step then resumed for twelve counts starting to the right, and finishing with the 'Break', preferably stamping with the left leg on the fourth count instead of swinging it forward.

Komarinskaia
Russian

Music and description in Burchenal's "Folk Dances and Singing Games."

Laudunum Bunches
English

Music and description in Burchenal's "Folk Dances and Singing Games."

St. Patrick's Day
Irish

Music and description in Burchenal's "Folk Dances and Singing Games."

Tarantella
Italian

Music and description in Burchenal's "Folk Dances and Singing Games."

Mallebrok
Danish

Formation: Couples

Measures 1 - 8   Social dancing position. Polka.
Partners face with hands on hips. Slide to the left, close right, slide left. Point right and clap hands.

,,   11 - 12   Repeat to the opposite.

,,   13 - 16   Eight jig steps in place. Jig step. Place left foot close behind right heel, hop left, bring right foot around behind left foot, hop right.

,,   9 - 16   Repeat slide, clap and jig.

Plain Quadrille

American

Plain Quadrille
Formation: Four couples facing in a hollow square.

Figure 1

"ADDRESS PARTNERS". . . . . .4 measures
   Partners bow to one another.

"ADDRESS CORNERS". 4   ,,
   Bow to neighbor

"FIRST FOUR RIGHT AND LEFT". 8   ,,
   Couples join nearest hands and cross over, ladies passing between the men.
   When in opposite place gentlemen turn ladies. Repeat back to place.

"BALANCE FOUR". 8   ,,
   Gentlemen cross hands with partners, slide to opposite place each passing
   to the right. Turn and return to place as before.

"LADIES CHAIN". 8   ,,
   Ladies cross to opposite place giving right hands as they pass. Joining left
   hands with opposite gentlemen they turn once and return to place as before.

"HALF PROMENADE". 4   ,,
   Join both hands crossed and slide to opposite place.

"HALF RIGHT AND LEFT". 4   ,,
   Return to places as in Right and Left

"ALL JOIN HANDS, FORWARD AND BACK". 4   ,,

"TURN PARTNERS". 4   ,,

Side couples repeat all movements.

Figure 2

Wait eight measures.

"FIRST TWO FORWARD AND SWING". . . . . .8 measures
   Head woman and opposite gentleman move forward to center, swing, and return to places.

"FOUR LADIES GRAND CHAIN". 8   ,,
   Ladies join right hands across, pinwheel fashion, walk half way round set,
   drop hands, turn opposite gentleman. Join right hands in center as before
   and return, turning partners in places.

"NEXT TWO FORWARD AND SWING". 8   ,,
   Head gentleman and opposite lady move forward and swing.

"FOUR GENTLEMEN GRAND CHAIN". 8   ,,

"NEXT TWO FORWARD AND SWING." 8   ,,
   Lady at left of head couple and opposite gentleman swing.

"LADIES GRAND CHAIN". 8   ,,

"LAST TWO FORWARD AND SWING". 8   ,,

"ALLEMANDE LEFT." 8   ,,
   Gentlemen swing lady on left.

"ALL PROMENADE". 8   ,,
   All cross hands with partners and promenade around circle.

Figure 3

Wait eight measures.

"FIRST FOUR CHASSE OUT AND FORM LINE". . . . . 8 measures
   Head couples join hands with partners, slide to right, forming line beside
   side couples.

"RIGHT AND LEFT". 8   ,,
   Couples immediately opposite execute the movement

"LADIES CHAIN". 8   ,,
   The same two couples.

"ALL JOIN HANDS, FORWARD AND BACK, TURN PARTNERS TO PLACE". . .8   ,,